Radiant
Raffia

Radiant
Raffia

20 Inspiring Crochet Projects made with Natural Yarn

Olga Panagopoulou

HERBERT PRESS

LONDON · OXFORD · NEW YORK · NEW DELHI · SYDNEY

For Electra

HERBERT PRESS
Bloomsbury Publishing Plc
50 Bedford Square, London,
WC1B 3DP, UK
29 Earlsfort Terrace,
Dublin 2, Ireland

BLOOMSBURY, HERBERT PRESS
and the Herbert Press logo are
trademarks of Bloomsbury
Publishing Plc

First published in Great Britain
in 2024

Bloomsbury Publishing Plc does
not have any control over, or
responsibility for, any third-party
websites referred to or in this book.
All internet addresses given in
this book were correct at the time
of going to press. The author and
publisher regret any inconvenience
caused if addresses have changed
or sites have ceased to exist, but
can accept no responsibility for
any such changes

A catalogue record for this book is
available from the British Library

ISBN: 978-1-7899-4198-2;
eBook: 978-1-7899-4197-5

10 9 8 7 6 5 4 3 2 1

Designed and typeset by
Austin Taylor
Printed and bound in China by RR Donnelle
Asia Printing Solutions Limited Company

MIX
Paper | Supporting
responsible forestry
FSC® C144853

To find out more about our
authors and books visit
www.bloomsbury.com and
sign up for our newsletters

CONTENTS

PART **1**
ACCESSORIES

PART **2**
HOMEWARES

PART **3**
SPECIAL STITCHES

INTRODUCTION

I was born in Athens where I lived and practised law for many years. Then, one day, I realised that what I wanted more than anything was to live closer to nature, and to spend my time crocheting.

I followed my heart, and now live happily on the dreamy Cycladic island of Syros, crocheting all day long. I'm surrounded by myriad colours, textures and materials, and can't help but let these settings and the seasonal changes inspire my patterns.

I am also lucky enough to be sharing these glorious experiences with my husband John and daughter Electra, who are always the first to evaluate my crocheting right there and then, our three cats – Raven, Tiger and Jessica – and Jason, our wise old dog.

I want to share my happiness and creativity with you. When making these patterns I hope you can imagine my island's skies, beaches and breezes, and the scents of its herbs and flowers, and that this book brings a little bit of the Cyclades to you.

I can be found on Instagram @plextopattern.

ABOUT THIS BOOK

This book is in two parts. Part 1 is dedicated to accessories, and Part 2 to homewares.

All the patterns are written in US crochet terms, and each one features a table with the corresponding UK terms. If you are new to reading crochet patterns or charts, you can find easy-to-follow instructions on pages 10–11.

Tutorials for all the special stitches featured can be found at the back of the book, after the projects, see pages 112–125.

WHAT IS RAFFIA?

Raffia in its natural form comes from the raffia palm tree, found mainly in Madagascar. It is actually the fibre produced from the membrane found on the underside of the leaf fronds, which is then dried. This fibre is used to make woven products, particularly carpets, baskets and even shoes. You can find natural raffia fibres in strands of about 1–1.30m/1–1.5yds, but this material is not suitable for fine crocheting as it is quite hard, and the end result would be rough and asymmetric.

below Natural raffia fibres

WHY WORK WITH RAFFIA YARN?

The material itself is a joy to work with – warm to the touch, pliable and raw. Its colours and textures echo my everyday environment – the roughness of the sand and rocks of the Cyclades, and the traditional objects used in daily life over the centuries. Crocheting with raffia warms my fingertips and my heart.

I recommend using a steel or aluminium crochet hook for these projects. The smoothness of metal hooks works well with the texture of the raffia.

A wide range of raffia yarns suitable for crocheting is available – some natural, some synthetic. In this book I use two types of raffia yarn, each of them perfect for a specific purpose. Both of them look a lot like natural raffia fibre. They are plant-based, eco-friendly, sustainable, biodegradable and ideal for crocheting.

See page 126 for a list of suppliers of the two types of yarn I use here.

above Wind your raffia tightly to help it regain its shape

below and right Raffia viscose yarn on cones

RAFFIA VISCOSE (25G; APPROX 55M/ 60.25YDS)

Raffia viscose is made of 100% viscose fibre. It is easy to work with and quite durable. It is soft to the touch, flexible and gives a beautiful end result. This material can be easily unravelled and, if you make a tight ball out of the loose yarn, it returns to its original shape and can be reused.

For projects made using this yarn, I recommend using a steam iron on a medium heat to set the shape of your finished objects.

above and right Raffia paper string

RAFFIA PAPER STRING
(100G; APPROX 150M/164YDS)

Raffia paper is made of 100% wood pulp. There are two types: single thread – which is not very durable so I do not recommend it for any of the projects in this book – and string, which is formed of two intertwined threads to make a durable yarn that is slightly rough. It is found in bundles which you need to turn into a ball.

It is rougher, tougher and definitely more difficult to crochet with than raffia viscose, but the end result is very stable and solid, making it ideal for decorative items such as vases and baskets, and pieces that need to stand on their own without the use of wires or other supports. The end product doesn't need to be ironed.

GIVING YOUR RAFFIA SOME TLC...

There are some things to keep in mind when it comes to cleaning your beautiful raffia objects, as each material has its own cleaning preferences!

Raffia viscose can be handwashed, but I advise doing so only when absolutely necessary and at a low temperature (not more than 30°C). When washed, it might lose its shape a bit, so it is better to avoid washing items where the shape and size are important – a hat, for instance. After washing, iron as recommended earlier. If you need to remove a stain, use a damp cloth to clean the area.

Raffia paper string should not come into contact with water at all, so it is better to use it for decorative items only. If necessary, gently clean with a damp cloth.

HOW TO READ A CROCHET PATTERN

To new crocheters, a pattern can look as if it's written in code. In fact, it is a code of sorts, but it's easy to decipher, and once you've worked a few rows you'll be following it easily.

Patterns are usually constructed in the same way, with rounds or rows, depending on whether you're working flat or in the round. These are some pattern components you will find in this book.

Each pattern starts with an instruction, usually to make a chain of a certain length. Here it's 2 chains.

A number and a stitch together (here it's 6sc) tells you how many of the type stitch to be worked – 6 single crochet stitches into one chain loop.

Often, the chain at the beginning of a row does not count as a stitch, but brings the yarn up to the height of the stitch (here it's Ch1, to match the single crochet).

Some chains at the beginning of a row do count as stitches, and this instruction tells you which ones.

This number in round brackets at the end of the row tells you how many stitches you should have.

This tells you which stitch to work into. Because the ch1 does not count as a stitch, you work this one into the first stitch of the row, to which the chain is attached.

Instructions between asterisks, like this, are repeated, usually to the end of the row or round.

Square brackets indicate a group of stitches, either to be repeated a number of times (similar to sets of instructions marked with an asterisk), or to be worked into one stitch, as in this example.

Often, a row will include different types of stitches and chain spaces. This row has 12 half-double crochet stitches, 6 spaces measuring 1 chain, and 6 spaces measuring 2 chains.

The instruction sk tells you to skip a certain number of stitches from the row below. Chains and chain spaces are never counted as stitches when skipping.

EXAMPLE PATTERN

Ch2.

Rnd 1: 6sc in second ch from the hook, slst into first sc. (6 sts)

Rnd 2: Ch1, 2sc in first st, 2sc in every stitch around, slst into first sc. (12 sts)

Rnd 3: Ch1, 1ws in first st, 2ws in next st, *1ws, 2ws in next st*, rpt from * to * around, slst into first ws. (18 sts)

Rnd 4: Ch3 (counts as 1hdc and ch1), 1hdc in first st, ch2, sk 2ws, *[1hdc, ch1, 1hdc] in next st, ch2, sk 2ws*, rpt from * to * around, slst into second ch, slst into third ch. (12 hdc, 6 ch1-sp, 6 ch2-sp)

HOW TO READ A CROCHET CHART

BASE CHART

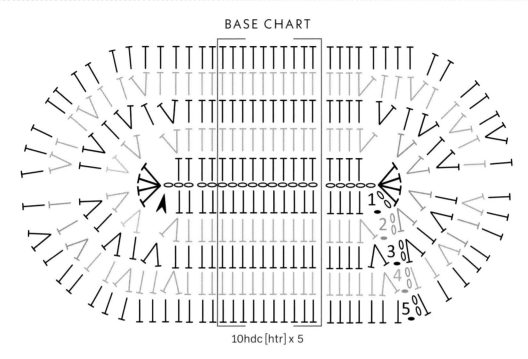

10hdc [htr] x 5

BAND CHART

The chart is a visual representation of the instructions – either the whole pattern or part of it (e.g. a repeated section). Reading them can take a little practice, but sometimes looking at the pattern chart can answer questions you might have about the written pattern.

Each symbol represents a stitch or other instruction. These are shown in the chart key for each pattern. The chart keys include both US and UK terminology – the UK terms are always inside square brackets.

For pieces worked back and forth in rows, an arrow will show the direction in which each row is worked. When working in the round, always read the chart anti-clockwise from the row number marker.

A red box surrounding a set of stitches or rows indicates that these stitches or rows are repeated.

KEY (US [UK])

➤	Start here
⤜	End of row
○	Chain
T	hdc [htr]
V	SPsc [SPdc]
↥	ws
•	Slip stitch (slst)
[ ]	Repeat

ABBREVIATIONS

US Abbreviation	US Description	UK Abbreviation	UK Description
Beg	Beginning/begin	Beg	Beginning/begin
Beg cross-tr	Beginning cross-treble crochet	Beg cross-dtr	Beginning cross-double treble crochet
CC	Contrasting colour	CC	Contrasting colour
ch	Chain	ch	Chain
ch-sp	Chain space	ch-sp	Chain space
cross-tr	Cross-treble crochet	cross-dtr	Cross-double treble crochet
dc	Double crochet	tr	Treble crochet
dc2tog	Double crochet 2 together	tr2tog	Treble crochet 2 together
dtr	Double treble crochet	trtr	Triple treble crochet
FPdc	Front post double crochet	FPtr	Front post treble crochet
FPhdc	Front post half-double crochet	FPhtr	Front post half-treble crochet
FPsc	Front post single crochet	FPdc	Front post double crochet
FPtr	Front post treble crochet	FPdtr	Front post double treble crochet
hdc	Half-double crochet	htr	Half-treble crochet
hdc2tog	Half-double crochet 2 together	htr2tog	Half-treble crochet 2 together
htr	Half-treble crochet	hdtr	Half-double treble crochet
MC	Main colour	MC	Main colour
PM	Place marker	PM	Place marker
Rnd	Round/s	Rnd	Round/s
Rpt	Repeat	Rpt	Repeat
RS	Right side of work	RS	Right side of work
sc	Single crochet	dc	Double crochet
sc2tog	Single crochet 2 together	dc2tog	Double crochet 2 together
sk	Skip	sk	Skip
slst	Slip stitch	slst	Slip stitch
SPsc	Spike stitch	SPdc	Spike stitch
st/s	Stitch/es	st/s	Stitch/es
tr	Treble crochet	dtr	Double treble crochet
trtr	Triple treble crochet	dtrtr	Double triple treble crochet
ws	Waistcoat stitch	ws	Waistcoat stitch
ws2tog	Waistcoat stitch 2 together	ws2tog	Waistcoat stitch 2 together

PART 1

ACCESSORIES

1

NET TOTE BAG

This roomy bag is perfect for the beach or the market. It's lightweight and easy to carry, and folds neatly into a small bundle when you're not using it. The pattern uses chains, half-double and treble stitches to build a flexible square mesh pattern that looks simple but stylish.

YOU WILL NEED

◈ Yarn: Raffia Viscose (210g; approx 462m/505yds)
◈ 3mm (No US equivalent – use C2 or D3/UK: 11)
◈ Tapestry needle
◈ Scissors

GAUGE

18 hdc and 10 rows = 10 x 10cm/4 x 4in

STITCHES

US	UK
ch	ch
slst	slst
hdc	htr
tr	dtr

FINAL SIZE

Height without handles: 52cm/20.5in
Total height: 82cm/32.25in
Width at base: 45cm/17.75in

SPECIAL NOTES

The Pattern has three parts:

1. Base
2. Body
3. Handles

The Base begins with a chain. The first round is worked up one side of the chain, then back down the opposite side. Each piece is worked consecutively – there is no need to bind off between sections.

The pattern is worked in joined rounds. Ch2 at the beginning of the round doesn't count as a stitch. Ch4 at the beginning of the round counts as first tr. Finish with slst to top of first hdc or to top of first ch4.

BASE CHART

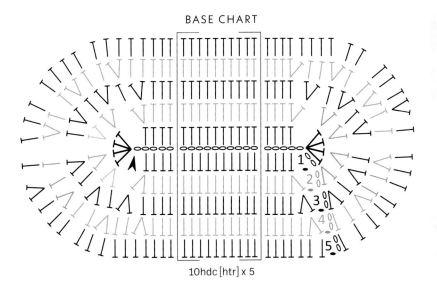

10hdc [htr] x 5

KEY (US [UK])

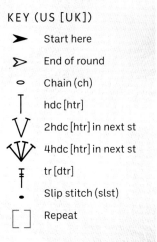

➤ Start here

➢ End of round

o Chain (ch)

T hdc [htr]

V 2hdc [htr] in next st

W 4hdc [htr] in next st

Ŧ tr [dtr]

• Slip stitch (slst)

[ ] Repeat

PATTERN

1. BASE

Ch62.

Rnd 1: 4hdc in third ch from hook, 58hdc, 4hdc in next ch, turn to work along the opposite side of the chain, 58hdc, slst into first hdc. (124 sts)

Rnd 2: Ch2, 2hdc in first st [2hdc in next st] 4 times, 56hdc, [2hdc in next st] 6 times, 56hdc, 2hdc in next st, slst into first hdc. (136 sts)

Rnd 3: Ch2, 2hdc in first st, 1hdc, [2hdc in next st, 1hdc] 4 times, 56hdc, [2hdc in next st, 1hdc] 6 times, 56hdc, 2hdc in next st, 1hdc, slst into first hdc. (148 sts)

Rnd 4: Ch2, 1hdc in first st, 1hdc, 2hdc in next st, [2hdc, 2hdc in next st] 4 times, 56hdc, [2hdc, 2hdc in next st] 6 times, 56hdc, 2hdc, 2hdc in next st, slst into first hdc. (160 sts)

Rnd 5: Ch2, 1hdc in first st, 8hdc, 2hdc in next st, 79hdc, 2hdc in next st, 70hdc, slst into first hdc. (162 sts)

2. BODY

Rnds 1–3: Ch2, 1hdc in every st around, slst into first hdc. (162 sts)

Rnd 4: Ch4 (counts as 1tr), 1tr, ch4, sk 4, *2tr, ch4, sk 4*, rpt from * to * around, slst into top of ch4. (54 sts, 27 ch4-sp)

Rnd 5: Ch2, 1hdc in first st, 1hdc, 4hdc in next ch4-sp, *2hdc, 4hdc in the next ch4-sp*, rpt from * to * around, slst into first hdc. (162 sts)

Rnds 6–27: Rpt Rnds 4–5 another 11 times.

Rnd 28: Slst around, slst into top of first hdc from Rnd 27.

3. HANDLES

Rnd 1: Slst33, ch100, sk 29, slst52, ch100, sk 29, slst18, slst into top of first hdc from Rnd 27. (304 sts)

Rnd 2: Ch2, 1 hdc in first st, 33hdc, 1hdc into each ch, 52hdc, 1hdc into each ch, 18hdc, slst into first hdc. (304 hdc)

Rnds 3–5: Slst around, slst into top of hdc from Rnd 2.

Fasten off securely and use tapestry needle to weave in ends.

BODY CHART

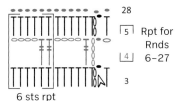

28

5 Rpt for Rnds 6–27

4

3

6 sts rpt

2

SHOULDER TOTE BAG

If you want to give the contents of your bag a little more protection
from the elements, this spacious shoulder tote is a great option. The pretty
diamond pattern is created using cleverly positioned chain spaces. It uses
two colours of raffia, which makes for a fun contrast.

YOU WILL NEED

◈ Yarn: Raffia Viscose
◈ MC: 140g; approx
308m/336.75yds
◈ CC: 110g; approx
242m/264.75yds
◈ 3mm (No US equivalent
– use C2 or D3/UK: 11)
◈ Tapestry needle
◈ Scissors

GAUGE

18 hdc and 10 rows
= 10 x 10cm/4 x 4in

FINAL SIZE

Height without handles:
42cm/17in
Total height: 65cm/25.5in
Width: 45cm/17.75in

STITCHES

US	UK
ch	ch
slst	slst
hdc	htr

SPECIAL NOTES

The Pattern has three parts:

1. Base
2. Body
3. Handles

The Base begins with a chain.
The first round is worked up
one side of the chain, then back
down the opposite side. Each
piece is worked consecutively

– there is no need to bind
off between sections.
After working the handles
you will twist the bag slightly
to centre them on either
side and straighten up the
diamond pattern.
The Pattern is worked in
joined rounds. Ch2 at the
beginning of the round
doesn't count as a stitch.

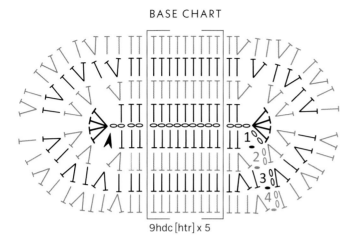

9hdc [htr] x 5

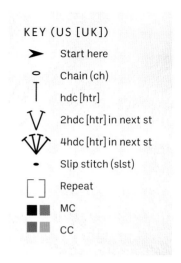
PATTERN

1. BASE

Using MC, ch54.

Rnd 1: 4hdc in third ch from hook, 50hdc, 4hdc in next st, turn to work along the opposite side of the chain, 50hdc, slst into first hdc. (108 sts)

Rnd 2: Ch2, 2hdc in first st, [2hdc in next st] 4 times, 48hdc, [2hdc in next st] 6 times, 48hdc, 2hdc in next st, slst into first hdc. (120 sts)

Rnd 3: Ch2, 2hdc in first st, 1hdc, [2hdc in next st, 1hdc] 4 times, 48hdc, [2hdc in next st, 1hdc] 6 times, 48hdc, 2hdc in next st, 1hdc, slst into first hdc. (132 sts)

Rnd 4: Ch2, 1hdc in first st, 1hdc, 2hdc in next st, [2hdc, 2hdc in next st] 4 times, 48hdc, [2hdc, 2hdc in next st] 6 times, 48hdc, 2hdc, 2hdc in next st, slst into first hdc. (144 sts)

2. BODY

After the first ch2 on each rnd, work the hdc into the first st.

Rnds 1–3: Ch2, 144hdc, slst into first hdc. (144 sts)

Rnd 4: Ch2, 144hdc, slst10.

Rnd 5: Ch2, *32hdc, ch4, sk 4hdc, 36hdc*, rpt from * to * once more, slst into first hdc. (136 hdc, 2 ch4-sp)

Rnd 6: Ch2, *31hdc, ch3, sk 1hdc, 1hdc into third ch, ch3, sk 2hdc, 34hdc*, rpt from * to * once more, slst into first hdc. (132 hdc, 4 ch3-sp)

Rnd 7: Ch2, *30hdc, ch3, sk 1hdc, 1hdc in third chain, 1hdc in next hdc, 1hdc in each of first 2 ch, ch3, sk 2hdc, 32hdc*, rpt from * to * once more, slst into first hdc.

Rnd 8: Ch2, *29hdc, ch3, sk 1hdc, 1hdc in third chain, 4hdc, 1hdc in each of first 2 ch, ch3, sk 2hdc, 30hdc*, rpt from * to * once more, slst into first hdc.

Rnd 9: Ch2, *28hdc, ch3, sk 1hdc, 1hdc in third ch, 7hdc, 1hdc in each of first 2 ch, ch3, sk 2hdc, 28hdc*, rpt from * to * once more, slst into first hdc.

Rnd 10: Ch2, *27hdc, ch3, sk 1hdc, 1hdc in third ch, 10hdc, 1hdc in each of first 2 ch, ch3, sk 2hdc, 26hdc*, rpt from * to * once more, slst into first hdc.

Rnd 11: Ch2, *26hdc, ch3, sk 1hdc, 1hdc in third ch, 13hdc, 1hdc in each of first 2 ch, ch3, sk 2hdc, 24hdc*, rpt from * to * once more, slst into first hdc.

Rnd 12: Ch2, *25hdc, ch3, sk 1hdc, 1hdc in third ch, 16hdc, 1hdc in each of first 2 ch, ch3, sk 2hdc, 22hdc*, rpt from * to * once more, slst into first hdc.

Rnd 13: Ch2, *24hdc, ch3, sk 1hdc, 1hdc in third ch, 19hdc, 1hdc in each of first 2 ch, ch3, sk 2hdc, 20hdc*, rpt from * to * once more, slst into first hdc.

BODY CHART

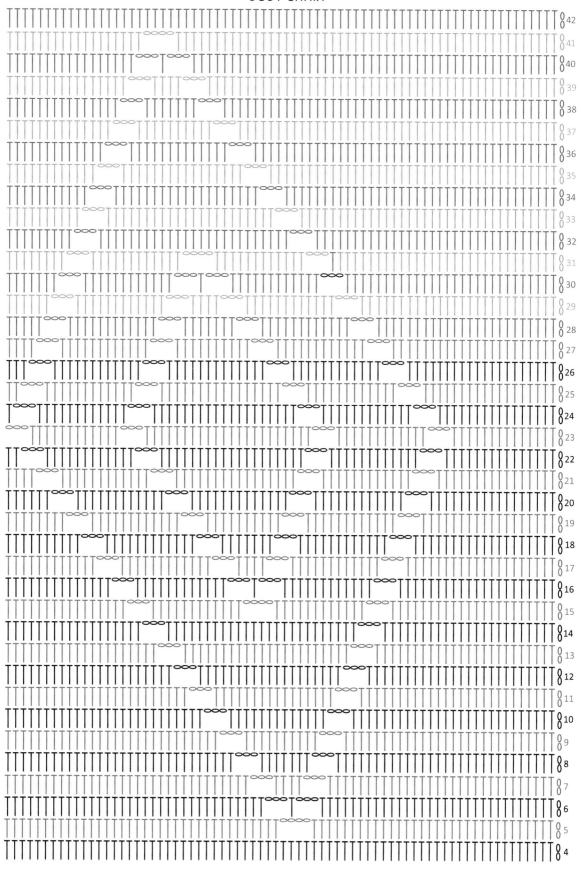

Rnd 14: Ch2, *23hdc, ch3, sk 1hdc, 1hdc in third ch, 22hdc, 1hdc in each of first 2 ch, ch3, sk 2hdc, 18hdc*, rpt from * to * once more, slst into first hdc.

Rnd 15: Ch2, *22hdc, ch3, sk 1hdc, 1hdc in third ch, 11hdc, ch4, sk 4hdc, 10hdc, 1hdc in each of first 2 ch, ch3, sk 2hdc, 16hdc*, rpt from * to * once more, slst into first hdc. (124 hdc, 4 ch3-sp, 2 ch4-sp)

Rnd 16: Ch2, *21hdc, ch3, sk 1hdc, 1hdc in third ch, 11hdc, ch3, sk 1hdc, 1hdc into third ch, ch3, sk 2hdc, 10hdc, 1hdc in each of first 2 ch, ch3, sk 2hdc, 14hdc*, rpt from * to * once more, slst into first hdc. (120 hdc, 8 ch3-sp)

Rnd 17: Ch2, *20hdc, ch3, sk 1hdc, 1hdc in third ch, 11hdc, ch3, sk 1hdc, 1hdc into third ch, 1hdc into next hdc, 1hdc in each of first 2 ch, ch3, sk 2hdc, 10hdc, 1hdc in each of first 2 ch, ch3, sk 2hdc, 12hdc*, rpt from * to * once more, slst into first hdc.

Rnd 18: Ch2, *19hdc, ch3, sk 1hdc, 1hdc in third ch, 11hdc, ch3, sk 1hdc, 1hdc in third ch, 4hdc, 1hdc in each of first 2 ch, ch3, sk 2hdc, 10hdc, 1hdc in each of first 2 ch, ch3, sk 2hdc, 10hdc*, rpt from * to * once more, slst into first hdc.

Rnd 19: Ch2, *18hdc, ch3, sk 1hdc, 1hdc in third ch, 11hdc, ch3, sk 1hdc, 1hdc in third ch, 7hdc, 1hdc in each of first 2 ch, ch3, sk 2hdc, 10hdc, 1hdc in

each of first 2 ch, ch3, sk 2hdc, 8hdc*, rpt from * to * once more, slst into first hdc.

Rnd 20: Ch2, *17hdc, ch3, sk 1hdc, 1hdc in third ch, 11hdc, ch3, sk 1hdc, 1hdc in third ch, 10hdc, 1hdc in each of first 2 ch, ch3, sk 2hdc, 10hdc, 1hdc in each of first 2 ch, ch3, sk 2hdc, 6hdc*, rpt from * to * once more, slst into first hdc.

Rnd 21: Ch2, *16hdc, ch3, sk 1hdc, 1hdc in third ch, 11hdc, ch3, sk 1hdc, 1hdc in third ch, 13hdc, 1hdc in each of first 2 ch, ch3, sk 2hdc, 10hdc, 1hdc in each of first 2 ch, ch3, sk 2hdc, 4hdc* rpt from * to * once more, slst into first hdc.

Rnd 22: Ch2, *15hdc, ch3, sk 1hdc, 1hdc in third ch, 11hdc, ch3, sk 1hdc, 1hdc in third ch, 16hdc, 1hdc in each of first 2 ch, ch3, sk 2hdc, 10hdc, 1hdc in each of first 2 ch, ch3, sk 2hdc, 2hdc*, rpt from * to * once more, slst into first hdc.

Rnd 23: Ch2, *14hdc, ch3, sk 1hdc, 1hdc in third ch, 11hdc, ch3, sk 1hdc, 1hdc in third ch, 19hdc, 1hdc in each of first 2 ch, ch3, sk 2hdc, 10hdc, 1hdc in each of first 2 ch, ch3, sk 2hdc*, rpt from * to * once more, slst into first hdc.

Rnd 24: Ch2 *14hdc, 1hdc in each of first 2 ch, ch3, sk 2hdc, 10hdc, 1hdc in each of first 2 ch, ch3, sk 2hdc, 19hdc, ch3, sk 1hdc, 1hdc in third ch, 11hdc, ch3, sk 1hdc, 1hdc in third ch*, rpt from * to * once more, slst into first hdc.

Rnd 25: Ch2, *16hdc, 1hdc in each of first 2 ch, ch3, sk 2hdc, 10hdc, 1hdc in each of first 2 ch, ch3, sk 2hdc, 16hdc, ch3, sk 1hdc, 1hdc in third ch, 11hdc, ch3, sk 1hdc, 1hdc in third ch, 1hdc*, rpt from * to * once more, slst into first hdc.

Rnd 26: Ch2, *18hdc, 1hdc in each of first 2 ch, ch3, sk 2hdc, 10hdc, 1hdc in each of first 2 ch, ch3, sk 2hdc, 13hdc, ch3, sk 1hdc, 1hdc in third ch, 11hdc, ch3, sk 1hdc, 1hdc in third ch, 2hdc*, rpt from * to * once more, slst into first hdc.

Rnd 27: Ch2, *20hdc, 1hdc in each of first 2 ch, ch3, sk 2hdc, 10hdc, 1hdc in each of first 2 ch, ch3, sk 2hdc, 10hdc, ch3, sk 1hdc, 1hdc in third ch, 11hdc, ch3, sk 1hdc, 1hdc in third ch, 3hdc*, rpt from * to * once more, slst into first hdc.

Break MC and join CC.

Rnd 28: Ch2, *22hdc, 1hdc in each of first 2 ch, ch3, sk 2hdc, 10hdc, 1hdc in each of first 2 ch, ch3, sk 2hdc, 7hdc, ch3, sk 1hdc, 1hdc in third ch, 11hdc, ch3, sk 1hdc, 1hdc in third ch, 4hdc*, rpt from * to * once more, slst into first hdc.

Rnd 29: Ch2, *24hdc, 1hdc in each of first 2 ch, ch3, sk 2hdc, 10hdc, 1hdc in each of first 2 ch, ch3, sk 2hdc, 4hdc, ch3, sk 1hdc, 1hdc in third ch, 11hdc, ch3, sk 1hdc, 1hdc in third ch, 5hdc*, rpt from * to * once more, slst into first hdc.

Rnd 30: Ch2, *26hdc, 1hdc in each of first 2 ch, ch3, sk 2hdc, 10hdc, 1hdc in each of first 2 ch, ch3, sk 2hdc, 1hdc, ch3, sk 1hdc, 1hdc in third ch, 11hdc, ch3, sk 1hdc, 1hdc in third ch, 6hdc*, rpt from * to * once more, slst into first hdc.

Rnd 31: Ch2, *28hdc, 1hdc in each of first 2 ch, ch3, sk 2hdc, 10hdc, 1hdc in each of first 2 ch, ch4, sk 1hdc, 1hdc in third ch, 11hdc, ch3, sk 1hdc, 1hdc in third ch, 7hdc*, rpt from * to * once more, slst into first hdc. (124 hdc, 4 ch3-sp, 2 ch4-sp)

Rnd 32: Ch2, *30hdc, 1hdc in each of first 2 ch, ch3, sk 2hdc, 10hdc, 1hdc in each ch, 11hdc, ch3, sk 1hdc, 1hdc in third ch, 8hdc*, rpt from * to * once more, slst into first hdc. (132 hdc, 4 ch3-sp)

Rnd 33: Ch2, *32hdc, 1hdc in each of first 2 ch, ch3, sk 2hdc, 22hdc, ch3, sk 1hdc, 1hdc in third ch, 9hdc*, rpt from * to * once more, slst into first hdc.

Rnd 34: Ch2, *34hdc, 1hdc in each of first 2 ch, ch3, sk 2hdc, 19hdc, ch3, sk 1hdc, 1hdc in third ch, 10hdc*, rpt from * to * once more, slst into first hdc.

Rnd 35: Ch2, *36hdc, 1hdc in each of first 2 ch, ch3, sk 2hdc, 16hdc, ch3, sk 1hdc, 1hdc in third ch, 11hdc*, rpt from * to * once more, slst into first hdc.

Rnd 36: Ch2, *38hdc, 1hdc in each of first 2 ch, ch3, sk 2hdc, 13hdc, ch3, sk 1hdc, 1hdc in third ch, 12hdc*, rpt from * to * once more, slst into first hdc.

Rnd 37: Ch2, *40hdc, 1hdc in each of first 2 ch, ch3, sk 2hdc, 10hdc, ch3, sk 1hdc, 1hdc in third ch, 13hdc*, rpt from * to * once more, slst into first hdc.

Rnd 38: Ch2, *42hdc, 1hdc in each of first 2 ch, ch3, sk 2hdc, 7hdc, ch3, sk 1hdc, 1hdc in third ch, 14hdc*, rpt from * to * once more, slst into first hdc.

Rnd 39: Ch2, *44hdc, 1hdc in each of first 2 ch, ch3, sk 2hdc, 4hdc, ch3, sk 1hdc, 1hdc in third ch, 15hdc*, rpt from * to * once more, slst into first hdc.

Rnd 40: Ch2, *46hdc, 1hdc in each of first 2 ch, ch3, sk 2hdc, 1hdc, ch3, sk 1hdc, 1hdc in third ch, 16hdc*, rpt from * to * once more, slst into first hdc.

Rnd 41: Ch2, *48hdc, 1hdc in each of first 2 ch, ch4, sk 1hdc, 1hdc in third ch, 17hdc*, rpt from * to * once more, slst into first hdc. (136 hdc, 2 ch4-sp)

Rnd 42: Ch2, *50hdc, 1hdc in each ch, 18hdc, slst into first hdc. (144 hdc)

3. HANDLES

Rnd 1: Slst around. (144 slst)

Rnd 2: *Slst34, ch80, sk 36, slst2*, rpt from * to * once more, slst into top of first hdc from Rnd 42. (72slst, 2 ch80)

Rnd 3: Ch2, *1hdc in first st, 33hdc, 1hdc in each ch, 2hdc*, rpt from *to* once more.

Rnd 4: Slst around, slst into top of first hdc from Rnd 3.

Rnd 5: Ch2, 1hdc in every st around.

Rnds 6–8: Rpt Rnd 4 another 3 times.

FINISHING

Fasten off securely and weave in ends. Place the bag on a flat surface and pin each corner of the base in place. Twist the top of the bag so that the handles are centralised. Steam it gently to set the shape.

3

DRAWSTRING BAG

This handy, lightweight drawstring bag has a long strap for wearing over the shoulder or across the body. It uses waistcoat stitch for the base, which looks great as well as being sturdy and stable. The cross-treble stitches are fun to work and create an attractive mesh section in the middle of the bag. If you want to reduce the mesh section, simply work more waistcoat stitch rows at the start of the Body section, and fewer rows of the cross-treble mesh.

YOU WILL NEED

- Yarn: Raffia Viscose
- MC: 85g; approx 187m/204.5yds
- CC: 75g; approx 165m/180.5yds
- Crochet hooks: 3mm (No US equivalent – use C2 or D3/UK: 11), 5mm (US: H8/UK: 6)
- 5mm (US: H8/UK: 6)
- Stitch marker
- Tapestry needle
- Scissors

GAUGE

16 ws and 18 rows
   = 10 x 10cm/4 x 4in using
   3mm hook
Each cross-treble row
   = 5cm/2in

FINAL SIZE

Height without handles:
   25.5cm/10in
Total handle length:
   59.5cm/23.5in
Diameter of the base:
   17.75cm/7in

STITCHES

US	UK
ch	ch
slst	slst
sc	dc

Special stitches (see pages 117–118 for tutorials).

ws	ws
beg cross-tr	beg cross-dtr
cross-tr	cross-dtr

SPECIAL NOTES

The Pattern has four parts:

1. Base
2. Body
3. Handle
4. Drawstring

The Base is worked in spiral rounds without slst to the beginning of the round.

The Body is worked from Rnds 1–12 in spiral rounds without slst to the beginning of the round, from Rnds 13–17 in joined rounds with slst to the top of the beg cross-tr, and from Rnds 18–31 in spiral rounds without slst to the beginning of the round.

The Handle is worked in rows.

PATTERN

When working in spiral rounds, PM in the first st to keep your place, and move the marker up every round as you work.

BASE CHART

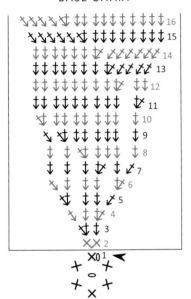

1. BASE

Using MC, ch2.

Rnd 1: 6sc into the second ch from hook. (6 sts)

Rnd 2: 2sc in every st around. (12 sts)

Rnd 3: *1ws, 2ws in next st*, rpt from * to * around. (18 sts)

Rnd 4: *2ws in next st, 2ws*, rpt from * to * around. (24 sts)

Rnd 5: *3ws, 2ws in next st*, rpt from * to * around. (30 sts)

Rnd 6: *2ws in next st, 4ws*, rpt from * to * around. (36 sts)

Rnd 7: *2ws, 2ws in next st, 3ws*, rpt from * to * around. (42 sts)

Rnd 8: *4ws, 2ws in next st, 2ws*, rpt from * to * around. (48 sts)

Rnd 9: *6ws, 2ws in next st, 1ws*, rpt from * to * around. (54 sts)

Rnd 10: *8ws, 2ws in next st*, rpt from * to * around. (60 sts)

Rnd 11: *2ws in next st, 9ws*, rpt from * to * around. (66 sts)

Rnd 12: *2ws, 2ws in next st, 8ws*, rpt from * to * around. (72 sts)

Rnd 13: *4ws, 2ws in next st, 7ws*, rpt from * to * around. (78 sts)

Rnd 14: *6ws, 2ws in next st, 6ws*, rpt from * to * around. (84 sts)

Rnd 15: *8ws, 2ws in next st, 5ws*, rpt from * to * around. (90 sts)

Rnd 16: *10ws, 2ws in next st, 4ws*, rpt from * to * around. (96 sts)

BODY CHART

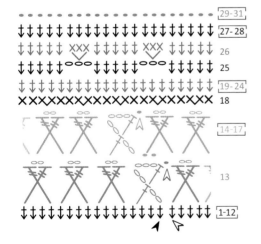

KEY (US [UK])

➤	Start here	[ ]	Repeat
➢	End of round	▪▪	MC
○	Chain (ch)	▪▪	CC
↨	ws		
ⱴ	2 ws in next st		
✕	sc [dc]		
✕✕	2sc [dc] in next st		
✕✕✕	3sc [dc] in next ch-sp		
	Beg cross-tr [beg cross-dtr]		
	Cross-tr [cross-dtr]		
•	Slip stitch (slst)		

2. BODY

Rnds 1–12: Using MC, 1ws in every st around. (96 sts)

Break MC and join CC.

Rnd 13: Using CC, beg cross-tr, cross-tr around, slst into first tr. (24 cross-tr)

Rnd 14: Slst2, beg cross-tr, cross-tr around, slst to join.

Rnds 15–17: Rpt Rnd 14 another 3 times.

Join MC.

Rnd 18 (MC): 1sc in first st, 2sc in ch2-sp, 1sc, *1sc, 2sc in next ch2-sp, 1sc*, rpt from * to * around. (96 sts)

Rnds 19–24: 1ws in every st around.

Rnd 25: *5ws, ch3, sk 3*, rpt from * to * around. (60 ws, 12 ch3-sp)

Rnd 26: *5ws, 3sc into the ch3-sp*, rpt from * to * around. (60 ws, 36 sc)

Rnds 27–28: 1ws in every st around. (96 sts)

Rnds 29–31: Using CC, slst around.

Fasten off securely and weave in ends.

3. HANDLE

Using MC, ch191 leaving a 20cm/8in tail. You will use this to attach the handle to the bag.

Row 1: 1sc in second ch from hook, 1sc in every ch, turn. (190 sts)

Row 2: Slst in every st around, turn.

Row 3: Ch1, 1sc in first stitch, 1sc in every st around, turn.

Rows 4–5: Rpt Rows 2–3 once more.

Row 6: Using CC, Rpt Row 2.

Fasten off, leaving a 20cm/8in tail. Using a tapestry needle and the tails at each end, attach the handle to the inside of the body at Round 28.

4. DRAWSTRING

Cut 3 lengths of CC, 3.9m/4.25yds long. Holding all 3 lengths of yarn together, make a slip knot. Using a 5mm crochet hook, ch100. Fasten off the chain and trim the ends. Thread the rope through the 3ch-sp you made in Round 25.

≈ 4 ≈

CELTIC WEAVE HANDBAG

This cute handbag uses the Celtic Weave stitch – crossed front post trebles – in the round. The raffia combined with the stitch gives a lovely basket-weave effect. Using this stitch also makes the base of the bag wider than the body, which gives it a distinctive, eye-catching shape. Simple waistcoat stitch is used for the base and the handles.

YOU WILL NEED

- Yarn: Raffia Viscose (180g; approx 396m/433yds)
- Crochet hook: 3mm (No US equivalent – use C2 or D3/UK: 11)
- Stitch marker
- Tapestry needle
- Scissors

GAUGE

16 ws and 18 rows
= 10 x 10cm/4 x 4in
10 rows of Celtic Weave st
= 10cm/4in

STITCHES

US	UK
ch	ch
slst	slst
sc	dc
hdc	dtr

Special stitches (see pages 114–125 for tutorials).

FPhdc	FPhtr
FPtr	FPdtr
ws	ws
Celtic Weave st	Celtic Weave st

FINAL SIZE

Height without handles:
21cm/8.25in
Total height: 25cm/9.75in
Width at base: 30cm/11.75in

SPECIAL NOTES

The Pattern has three parts:

1. Base
2. Body
3. Handles

The Base begins with a chain. The first round is worked up one side of the chain, then back down the opposite side. Each piece is worked consecutively – there is no need to bind off between sections.

The Base and Handles are worked in spiral rounds without slst to the beginning of the round.

The Body is worked in joined rounds. Ch1, ch2 or ch3 at the beginning of the round doesn't count as a st. Work the last FP st around both the last st and the first ch2 or ch3 of the previous round.

PATTERN

1. BASE

When working in spiral rounds, PM in the first st to keep your place, and move the marker up every round as you work.

Ch27.

Rnd 1: 3sc in second ch from hook, 24sc, 3sc in next st, turn to work along the opposite side of the chain, 24sc. (54 sts)

Rnd 2: *[2ws in next st] 3 times, 24ws*, rpt from * to * once more. (60 sts)

Rnd 3: *[1ws, 2ws in next st] 3 times, 24ws*, rpt from * to * once more. (66 sts)

Rnd 4: *[2ws in next st, 2ws] 3 times, 24ws*, rpt from * to * once more. (72 sts)

Rnd 5: *[2ws, 2ws in next st, 1ws] 3 times, 24ws*, rpt from * to * once more. (78 sts)

Rnd 6: *[4ws, 2ws in next st] 3 times, 24ws*, rpt from * to * once more. (84 sts)

Rnd 7: *[2ws in next st, 5ws] 3 times, 24ws*, rpt from * to * once more. (90 sts)

Rnd 8: *[2ws, 2ws in next st, 4ws] 3 times, 24ws*, rpt from * to * once more. (96 sts)

Rnds 9–11: 1ws in every st around.

2. BODY

Rnd 1: Ch2, 1hdc in first st, hdc around, slst into first hdc. (96 hdc)

Rnd 2: Ch3, *sk 2hdc, 2FPtr, cross behind sts just made, 1FPtr around first sk st, 1FPtr around second sk st*, rpt from * to * around, slst into first FPtr.

Place Celtic Weave Pattern as follows:

Rnd 3: Ch3, sk first 4 sts of last rnd, 2FPtr, cross in front of sts just made, 1FPtr around third sk st, 1FPtr around fourth sk st, *sk 2FPtr, 2FPtr, cross in front

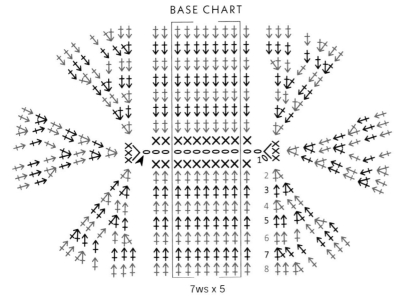

BASE CHART

7ws x 5

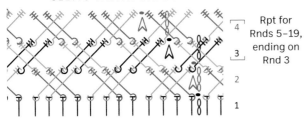

CELTIC WEAVE CHART

Rpt for Rnds 5–19, ending on Rnd 3

KEY (US [UK])

➤	Start here
➢	End of round
o	Chain (ch)
✕	sc [dc]
✕✕✕	3sc [dc] in next st
↓	ws
⩔	2ws in next st
⊤	hdc [htr]
⌇	FPtr [FPdtr] behind
⌇⌇	FPtr [FPdtr] in front
•	Slip stitch (slst)
[ ]	Repeat

of sts just made, 1FPtr around first sk st, 1FPtr around second sk st*, rpt from * to * until 2 sts rem, sk 2FPtr, 1FPtr around first st from last rnd, 1FPtr around second sts from last rnd, cross in front of sts just made, 1FPtr around first sk st, 1FPtr around second sk st, slst into first FPtr.

Rnd 4: Ch3, sk first 4 sts of last rnd, 2FPtr, cross behind sts just made, 1FPtr around third sk st, 1FPtr around fourth sk st, *sk 2FPtr, 2FPtr, cross behind sts just made, 1FPtr around first sk st, 1FPtr around second sk st*, rpt from * to * until 2 sts rem, sk 2FPtr, 1FPtr around first st from last rnd, 1FPtr around second st from last rnd,

cross behind sts just made, 1FPtr around first sk st, 1FPtr around second sk st, slst into first FPtr.

Rnds 5–19: Rpt Rnds 3–4 another 7 times, then work Rnd 3 once more.

Fasten off securely.

Count 12 sts from where you fastened off – this will bring you to the centre of one side, to the second st of a 4-st cross. Reattach yarn in the top of the next FPtr.

Rnd 20: Ch2, 1FPhdc in every st around, slst into first FPhdc. (96 sts)

Rnd 21: Ch1, 1sc in every st around, slst into first sc.

3. HANDLES

Rnds 1–2: 1ws in every st around. (96 sts)

Rnd 3: Slst around, slst into top of first ws from Rnd 2.

Rnd 4: Slst15, ch20, sk 16, slst32, ch20, sk 16, slst16. (104 sts)

Rnd 5: 16sc, 1sc into each ch, 32sc, 1sc into each ch, 16sc.

Rnds 6–7: Rpt Rnds 1–2 once more.

Rnds 8–10: Rpt Rnd 3 another 3 times.

Fasten off securely and weave in ends.

≈ 5 ≈
SPIKE STITCH HANDBAG

This pretty bag uses waistcoat and spike stitches in two colours to great effect. It has a beautiful texture, and its wide base and sturdy body means it will stand upright. The handles are solid, so you can slip it over your arm easily and still have easy access to your things. It would make a perfect project bag!

YOU WILL NEED

- Yarn: Raffia Viscose
- MC: 110g; approx 242m/264.75yds
- CC: 50g; approx 125m/136.75yds
- Crochet hook: 3mm (No US equivalent – use C2 or D3/UK: 11)
- Tapestry needle
- Stitch marker
- Scissors

GAUGE

16 ws and 18 rows
  = 10 x 10cm/4 x 4in
22 spike stitch pattern rows
  = 10cm/4in

FINAL SIZE

Height without handles:
  18cm/7in
Total height: 26cm/10.25in
Width: 30cm/11.75in

STITCHES

US	UK
ch	ch
slst	slst

Special stitches (see pages 124–125 for tutorials).

SPsc	SPdc
ws	ws

SPECIAL NOTES

The Pattern has three parts:

1. Base
2. Body
3. Handles

The base and the body are worked consecutively in spiral rounds without slst to the beginning of the round. The handles are worked separately in rows and spiral rounds.

PATTERN

When working in spiral rounds, PM in the first st to keep your place, and move the marker up every round as you work.

1. BASE

Using MC, ch21.

Rnd 1: 3sc in second ch from hook, 18sc, 3sc in next st, turn to work along the opposite side of the chain, 18sc. (42sc)

Rnd 2: *[2ws in next st] 3 times, 18ws*, rpt from * to * once more. (48 sts)

Rnd 3: *[1ws, 2ws in next st] 3 times, 18ws*, rpt from * to * once more. (54 sts)

Rnd 4: *[2ws in next st, 2ws] 3 times, 18ws*, rpt from * to * once more. (60 sts)

Rnd 5: *[2ws, 2ws in next st, 1ws] 3 times, 18ws*, rpt from * to * once more. (66 sts)

Rnd 6: *[4ws, 2ws in next st] 3 times, 18ws*, rpt from * to * once more. (72 sts)

Rnd 7: *[2ws in next st, 5ws] 3 times, 18ws*, rpt from * to * once more. (78 sts)

Rnd 8: *[2ws, 2ws in next st, 4ws] 3 times, 18ws*, rpt from * to * once more. (84 sts)

Rnd 9: *[4ws, 2ws in next st, 3ws] 3 times, 18ws*, rpt from * to * once more. (90 sts)

Rnd 10: *[6ws, 2ws in next st, 2ws] 3 times, 18ws*, rpt from * to * once more. (96 sts)

2. BODY

Rnd 1: 1ws in every st around. (96 sts)

Rnd 2: 1sc in every st around.

Rnd 3: 1SPsc into first st, 1sc, *1SPsc, 1sc*, rpt from * to * around.

Join CC. Do not break MC.

Rnd 4: Using CC, 1sc into first st, 1SPsc, *1sc, 1SPsc*, rpt from * to * around.

Rnd 5: Using MC, 1SPsc into first st, 1sc, *1SPsc, 1sc*, rpt from * to * around.

Rnds 6–27: Rpt Rnds 4–5 another 11 times.

Break CC and fasten off. Continue using MC only.

KEY (US [UK])

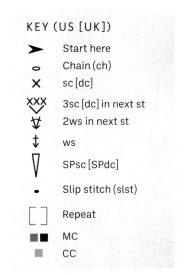

➤	Start here
o	Chain (ch)
✕	sc [dc]
✕✕✕	3sc [dc] in next st
⊻	2ws in next st
‡	ws
▽	SPsc [SPdc]
•	Slip stitch (slst)
[ ]	Repeat
■ ■	MC
▨	CC

BODY CHART

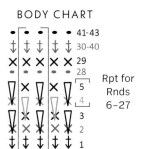

Rpt for Rnds 6–27

BASE CHART

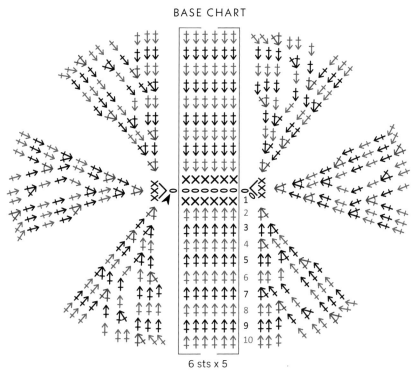

6 sts x 5

Rnd 28: Slst around.

Rnd 29: Rpt Rnd 2.

Rnds 30-40: Rpt Rnd 1 another 11 times.

Rnds 41-43: Rpt Rnd 28 another 3 times.

Fasten off MC and weave in ends.

3. HANDLES (MAKE 2)

Leave a long tail at the beginning and at the end. You will use these to attach the handles to the body later on. You will work the handles back and forth in rows for Rows 1–4. You will then join to work in the round for Rnds 5–44, and then back and forth in rows again for Rows 45–48.

Ch9.

Row 1: Sc in second ch from hook, 7sc, turn. (8 sts)

Rows 2-4: Ch1, 1sc in first st, 7sc, turn.

Rnd 5: Ch1, 1sc into first st, 7sc, slst to the first sc.

Rnds 6-44: 1sc into first st, 7sc.

Row 45: 8sc, turn.

Rows 46-48: Ch1, 1sc in first st, 7sc, turn.

Fasten off securely.

Using a tapestry needle and the long tails at each end, attach each handle to the inside of the bag, placing the ends 8cm/3.25in either side of the centre.

≈6≈

SUMMER HAT

Who doesn't love a shady hat for the beach or a summer stroll? This one-size hat uses simple waistcoat stitch to give it structure. It can be easily fitted to any head size using a ribbon. I suggest using a bundle of raffia strings for this, but you can use any ribbon – it's endlessly customisable.

STITCHES

US	UK
ch	ch
slst	slst
sc	dc

Special stitch (see page 125 for tutorial).

ws	ws

SPECIAL NOTES

The Pattern has three parts:

1. Crown
2. Brim
3. Ribbon

The Crown and Brim are worked in spiral rounds without slip stitching to the beginning of the round, and there is no need to fasten off between sections. The ribbon is worked in a contrasting raffia viscose yarn.

YOU WILL NEED

◉ Yarn: Raffia Viscose (155g; approx 341m/373yds)
◉ If you are using a contrasting colour of raffia viscose for the ribbon, you will need about 3g (approx 6.5m/7.25yds)
◉ Crochet hook: 3mm (No US equivalent – use C2 or D3/UK: 11)
◉ Stitch marker
◉ Tapestry needle
◉ Scissors

GAUGE

16 ws and 18 rows = 10 x 10cm/4 x 4in

FINAL SIZE

Crown circumference: 60cm/23.5in
Crown height: 8.5cm/3.25in
Brim width: 8.5cm/3.25in

PATTERN

When working in spiral rounds, PM in the first st to keep your place, and move the marker up every round as you work.

1. CROWN

Ch2.

Rnd 1: 6sc in second ch from hook, slst into the first sc. (6 sts)

Rnd 2: *2sc in next st*, rpt from * to * around. (12 sts)

Rnd 3: *1ws, 2ws in next st*, rpt from * to * around. (18 sts)

Rnd 4: *2ws in next st, 2ws*, rpt from * to * around. (24 sts)

Rnd 5: *3ws, 2ws in next st*, rpt from * to * around. (30 sts)

Rnd 6: *2ws in next st, 4ws*, rpt from * to * around. (36 sts)

Rnd 7: *2ws, 2ws in next st, 3ws*, rpt from * to * around. (42 sts)

Rnd 8: *4ws, 2ws in next st, 2ws*, rpt from * to * around. (48 sts)

Rnd 9: *6ws, 2ws in next st, 1ws*, rpt from * to * around. (54 sts)

Rnd 10: *8ws, 2ws in next st*, rpt from * to * around. (60 sts)

Rnd 11: *2ws in next st, 9ws*, rpt from * to * around. (66 sts)

Rnd 12: *2ws, 2ws in next st, 8ws*, rpt from * to * around. (72 sts)

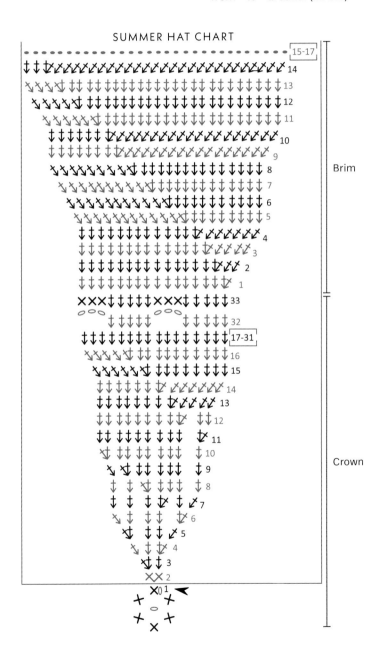

SUMMER HAT CHART

Brim

Crown

KEY (US [UK])

➤ Start here

➢ End of round

o Chain (ch)

↧ ws

Ѵ̵ 2ws in next st

✕ sc [dc]

✕✕ 2sc [dc] in next st

• Slip stitch (slst)

[ ] Repeat

Rnd 13: *4ws, 2ws in next st, 7ws*, rpt from * to * around. (78 sts)

Rnd 14: *6ws, 2ws in next st, 6ws*, rpt from * to * around. (84 sts)

Rnd 15: *8ws, 2ws in next st, 5ws*, rpt from * to * around. (90 sts)

Rnd 16: *10ws, 2ws in next st, 4ws*, rpt from * to * around. (96 sts)

Rnds 17–31: 1ws in every st around. (96 sts)

Rnd 32: *5ws, ch3, sk 3*, rpt from * to * around. (60 sts, 12 ch3-sp)

Rnd 33: *5ws, 3sc in the ch3-sp*, rpt from * to * around. (96 sts)

2. BRIM

Rnd 1: *2ws in next st, 15ws*, rpt from * to * around. (102 sts)

Rnd 2: *2ws, 2ws in next st, 14ws*, rpt from * to * around. (108 sts)

Rnd 3: *4ws, 2ws in next st, 13ws*, rpt from * to * around. (114 sts)

Rnd 4: *6ws, 2ws in next st, 12ws*, rpt from * to * around. (120 sts)

Rnd 5: *8ws, 2ws in next st, 11ws*, rpt from * to * around. (126 sts)

Rnd 6: *10ws, 2ws in next st, 10ws*, rpt from * to * around. (132 sts)

Rnd 7: *12ws, 2ws in next st, 9ws*, rpt from * to * around. (138 sts)

Rnd 8: *14ws, 2ws in next st, 8ws*, rpt from * to * around. (144 sts)

Rnd 9: *16ws, 2ws in next st, 7ws*, rpt from * to * around. (150 sts)

Rnd 10: *18ws, 2ws in next st, 6ws*, rpt from * to * around. (156 sts)

Rnd 11: *20ws, 2ws in next st, 5ws*, rpt from * to * around. (162 sts)

Rnd 12: *22ws, 2ws in next st, 4ws*, rpt from * to * around. (168 sts)

Rnd 13: *24ws, 2ws in next st, 3ws*, rpt from * to * around. (174 sts)

Rnd 14: *26ws, 2ws in next st, 2ws*, rpt from * to * around. (180 sts)

Rnds 15–17: Slst around.

3. RIBBON

Cut 6 lengths of raffia viscose yarn, 110cm/43.5in long, and make a small bundle. Thread it through the spaces formed on Round 32 of the crown and adjust it to fit comfortably.

Fasten off securely and weave in ends.

CELTIC WEAVE CUFF

Make a statement with this chunky cuff. It uses the Celtic Weave stitch in two colours to create a deceptively complex pattern, which stands out even more thanks to the textured raffia.

YOU WILL NEED

- Yarn: Raffia Viscose
- MC: 15g; approx 33m/36yds
- CC: 10g; approx 22m/24yds
- Crochet hook: 3mm (No US equivalent – use C2 or D3/UK: 11)
- Tapestry needle
- Stitch marker
- Scissors

GAUGE

18 hdc and 10 rows
   = 10 x 10cm/4 x 4in
2 rows of Celtic Weave pattern
   = 2cm/0.75in

FINAL SIZE

Width: 7.5cm/3in
Length: 12cm/4.75in

STITCHES

US	UK
ch	ch
slst	slst
sc	dc
sc2tog	dc2tog
hdc	dtr

Special stitches (see pages 114–121 for tutorials).

FPhdc	FPhtr
FPtr	FPdtr
Celtic Weave st	Celtic Weave st

SPECIAL NOTES

You can adjust the size of the cuff by working fewer or more chains (in multiples of 7). Each set of 7 sts adds approximately 3.75cm/1.5in to the circumference.

The Pattern is worked in joined rounds. Ch1, ch2 or ch3 at the beginning of the round doesn't count as a stitch.

When working Celtic Weave pattern, work the last FPtr around the last stitch and the first ch2 or ch3 of the previous round.

PATTERN

Using MC, ch42, slst to join to the first ch.

Rnd 1: Ch1, 1sc in every ch around, slst into first sc. (42 sts)

Rnd 2: (MC) Ch2, 1hdc in first st, 1hdc, (CC) 2hdc, (MC) 2hdc, (CC) 2hdc in next st, *(MC) 2hdc, (CC) 2hdc, (MC) 2hdc, (CC) 2hdc in next st*, rpt from * to * around, slst into first hdc. (48 sts)

Rnd 3: (MC) Ch3, *sk 2hdc, (CC) 2FPtr, cross behind sts just made, (MC) 1FPtr around first sk st, 1FPtr around second sk st*, rpt from * to * around, slst into first FPtr.

Rnd 4: (MC) Ch3, sk first 4 sts of last rnd, (CC) 2FPtr, (MC) cross in front of sts just made, 1FPtr around third sk st, 1FPtr around fourth sk st, *sk 2FPtr, (CC) 2FPtr, (MC) cross in front

of sts just made, 1FPtr around first sk st, 1FPtr around second sk st*, rpt from * to * until 2 sts rem, sk 2, (CC) 1FPtr around first st from last rnd, 1FPtr around second st from last rnd, (MC) cross in front of sts just made, 1FPtr around first sk st, 1FPtr around second sk st, slst into first FPtr.

Rnd 5: (MC) Ch3, sk first 4 sts of last rnd, (CC) 2FPtr, (MC) cross behind sts just made, 1FPtr around third sk st, 1FPtr around fourth sk st, *sk 2FPtr, (CC) 2FPtr, (MC) cross behind sts just made, 1FPtr around first sk st, 1FPtr around second sk st*, rpt from * to * until 2 sts rem, sk 2FPtr, (CC) 1FPtr around first st from last rnd, 1FPtr around second st from last rnd, (MC) cross behind sts just made, 1FPtr around first sk st, 1FPtr around second sk st, slst into first FPtr.

Rnd 6: (MC) Ch2, (CC) 1FPhdc around first st, 1FPhdc, (MC) 2FPhdc, *(CC) 2FPhdc, (MC) 2FPhdc*, rpt from * to * around, slst into first FPhdc.

Rnd 7: Using MC, Ch1, 1sc in first st, 5sc, sc2tog, *6sc, sc2tog*, rpt from * to * around, slst into first sc. (42 sts)

Rnd 8: Using MC, slst around.

Rnd 9: Using CC, slst around.

Rnd 10: Rpt Rnd 8.

Fasten off.

Reattach MC in any st of the starting chain, on the opposite side to the edge just fastened off.

Rnd 11: Using MC, slst around.

Rnd 12: Using CC, slst around.

Rnd 13: Using MC, slst around.

Fasten off securely and weave in ends.

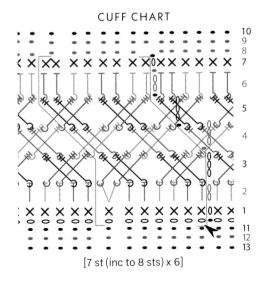

CUFF CHART

[7 st (inc to 8 sts) x 6]

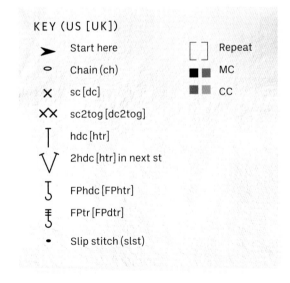

KEY (US [UK])

➤ Start here
o Chain (ch)
✕ sc [dc]
✕✕ sc2tog [dc2tog]
I hdc [htr]
V 2hdc [htr] in next st
FPhdc [FPhtr]
FPtr [FPdtr]
• Slip stitch (slst)

☐ Repeat
■ ■ MC
■ ■ CC

≈ 8 ≈
FLOWERY HEADBAND

This boho headband will bring out your inner flower child.
The ties at the back make it easily adjustable, so it's really comfortable
to wear, and perfect for a quick gift. I've used two flowers, but you can
add as many as you like. Make a whole bouquet!

YOU WILL NEED

◉ Yarn: Raffia Viscose
◉ MC: 61g; approx
134.25m/146.75yds
◉ CC: 12g; approx
26.50m/29yds
◉ Crochet hook: 3mm
(No US equivalent – use C2
or D3/UK: 11)
◉ Tapestry needle
◉ Scissors

GAUGE

16 ws and 18 rows
    = 10 x 10cm/4 x 4in
36 Spike stitch pattern rows
    = 10cm/4in

FINAL SIZE

Length: 50cm/19.5in
Width: 4cm/1.5in

STITCHES

US	UK
ch	ch
slst	slst

Special stitches (see pages
122–125 for tutorials).

SPsc	SPsc
Puff Petal	Puff Petal
ws	ws

SPECIAL NOTES

The Pattern has three parts:

1. Band
2. Tie strings
3. Flowers

The Band is worked in rows.
The Flower is worked in
joined rounds with slst to the
beginning of the round.

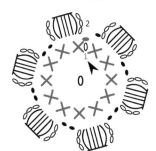

BAND CHART

→ 6
→ 4
→ 2
7
5
3
1

Rpt for Rows 8–183

FLOWER CHART

KEY (US [UK])

➤	Start here
o	Chain (ch)
✕	sc [dc]
•	Slip stitch (slst)
ⵏ	SPsc [SPdc]
ⵏ	ws
ⵚ	Puff petal
⇄	Direction of work
▢	Repeat

PATTERN

1. BAND

Using MC, ch10.

Row 1: 1sc in second ch from hook, 1sc in every ch across, turn. (9 sts)

Rows 2, 4 and 6: Slst across, turn.

Row 3: Ch1, 1SPsc in the base of first sc from Row 1, *1ws in the next sc from Row 1, 1SPsc in the base of the next sc from Row 1*, rpt from * to * to end, turn.

Row 5: Ch1, 1ws in first st, *1SPsc in the base of the next ws from Row 3, 1ws in the next SPsc from Row 3*, rpt from * to * to end, turn. (9 sts)

Row 7: Ch1, 1SPsc in the base of the first ws from Row 5, *1ws in the next SPsc from Row 5, 1SPsc in the base of the next ws from Row 5*, rpt from * to * to end, turn.

Rows 8–183: Rpt Rows 4–7 another 44 times.

Fasten off securely and weave in ends.

2. TIE STRINGS (MAKE 2)

Using MC, ch20, slst through the first chain and fasten off, leaving a 20cm/8in tail.

Using a tapestry needle and the tails left, attach the tie strings to the centre of each end of the band.

3. FLOWERS

Using CC, ch2.

Rnd 1: 12sc in second ch from hook, slst into first sc. (12 sc)

Rnd 2: Work Puff Petal into first 2 sts, *slst into next st, work Puff Petal into this and next st*, rpt from * to * another 4 times. (6 petals)

Fasten off securely and weave in ends. Using CC, and working through the centre of each flower, attach the flowers to the headband where you'd like them placed.

DISC BELT

You can customise this striking belt by experimenting with the number of discs you make and how you put them together. Try using contrasting colours of raffia to really mix things up.

YOU WILL NEED

- Yarn: Raffia Viscose (45g; approx 99m/108.25yds)
- Crochet hook: 3mm (No US equivalent – use C2 or D3/UK: 11)
- Tapestry needle
- Scissors

GAUGE

16 ws and 18 rows
  = 10 x 10cm/4 x 4in

FINAL SIZE

Disc A diameter: 2.5cm/1in
Disc B diameter: 4.5cm/1.75in
Discs C and D diameter:
  6.5cm/2.5in
Length: 96cm/37.75in
Width at widest point:
  6.5cm/2.5in

STITCHES

US	UK
ch	ch
slst	slst
sc	dc

Special stitch (see page 125 for tutorial).

ws	ws

SPECIAL NOTES

The Pattern gives instructions for four different discs of varying sizes.

After creating each disc, make sure to leave some extra thread on the end for stitching them together.

Every disc is worked in joined rounds. Ch1 at the beginning of the round doesn't count as a stitch.

PATTERN

DISC A (MAKE 12)

Ch8, slst into first st to form a ring.

Rnd 1: Ch1, 12sc into ring, slst into first sc. (12 sts)

Rnd 2: Slst around.

Fasten off, leaving a 10cm/4in tail.

DISC B (MAKE 6)

Ch2.

Rnd 1: 6sc in second ch from hook, slst into first sc. (6 sts)

DISC A CHART

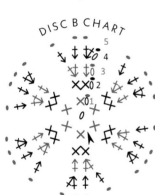

DISC B CHART

Rnd 2: Ch1, 2sc into every st around, slst into first sc. (12 sts)

Rnd 3: Ch1 and 1ws in first st, 2ws in next st, *1ws, 2ws in next st*, rpt from * to * around, slst into first ws. (18 sts)

Rnd 4: Ch1, 2ws in first st, 2ws, *2ws in next st, 2ws*, rpt from * to * around, slst into first ws. (24 sts)

Rnd 5: Slst around.

Fasten off, leaving a 10cm/4in tail.

DISC C (MAKE 3)

Ch20, slst into first ch to form a ring.

Rnd 1: Ch1, 36sc into ring, slst into first sc. (36 sts)

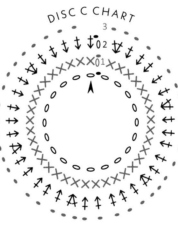

DISC C CHART

Rnd 2: Ch1, 1ws in first st, 4ws, 2ws in next st, *5ws, 2ws in next st*, rpt from * to * around, slst into first ws. (42 sts)

Rnd 3: Slst around.

Fasten off, leaving a 10cm/4in tail.

DISC D (MAKE 3)

Ch15, slst into first ch to form a ring.

Rnd 1: Ch1, 30sc into ring, slst into first sc. (30 sts)

Rnd 2: Ch1, 1sc in first st, 3sc, 2sc in next st, *4sc, 2sc in next st*, rpt from * to * around, slst into first sc. (36 ws)

Rnd 3: Ch1, 2ws in first st, 5ws, *2ws in next st, 5ws*, rpt from * to * around, slst into first ws. (42 sts)

Rnd 4: Slst around.

Fasten off, leaving a 10cm/4in tail.

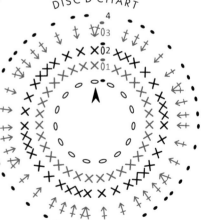

DISC D CHART

KEY (US [UK])

➤	Start here	↕	ws
○	Chain (ch)	⅄	2ws in next st
✕	sc [dc]	•	Slip stitch (slst)
✕✕	2sc [dc] in next st	[ ]	Repeat

FINISHING

Stitch the discs together as shown in Fig 1.

This is the first piece of the belt. Repeat twice more with the remaining circles. Your belt is now in three pieces. Stitch disc C of the first piece to disc A of the second piece, and disc C of the second piece to disc A of the third piece.

Fasten off securely and weave in ends.

Fig 1: Assembling your belt

CHAIN LOOP BELT

The Chain Loop stitch used in this belt is really fun to work, and creates a highly textured front with a smooth, comfortable back. It's a real statement piece – cinch it at the waist or wear it loosely around your hips for a casual look.

YOU WILL NEED

◎ Yarn: Raffia Viscose (65g; approx 143m/156.5yds)
◎ Crochet hook: 3mm (No US equivalent – use C2 or D3/UK: 11)
◎ Tapestry needle
◎ Scissors

GAUGE

16 sc x 18 rows = 10 x 10cm/ 4 x 4in

2 rows of Chain Loop pattern = 1cm/0.5in

FINAL SIZE

Length without clasp: 81cm /31.75in
Width: 6cm/2.5in
The clasp will add approx 5cm/ 2in to the total length of the belt

STITCHES

US	UK
ch	ch
slst	slst
sc	dc

Special stitches (see pages 116–125 for tutorials).

WS	WS
Chain loop st	Chain loop st

SPECIAL NOTES

The Pattern has two parts:

1. Band
2. Clasp

The band is worked back and forth in rows. When working the WS rows, keep the chain loops on the RS of your work and crochet in front of them. You can lengthen or shorten the belt by working more or fewer chains at the beginning in multiples of 2. Each 2sts meas approx 1.25cm/0.5in.

The clasp is made up of three discs – A, B and C – which are worked in joined rounds with slst joins at the end of each round.

PATTERN

1. BAND

Ch131.

Row 1 (WS): 1sc in second ch from hook, 1sc in every ch across, turn. (130 sts)

Row 2 (RS): Ch1, 1sc in first st, ch4, 1sc, *1sc, ch4, 1sc*, rpt from * to * across, turn. (130 sc, 65 ch4-loops)

Row 3: Ch1, keeping loops to the RS of the work, 1sc in top of each sc from row below, turn. (130 sts)

Row 4: Ch1, 1sc in first st, 1sc in next st, *ch4, 2sc*, rpt from * to * to end, turn. (130 sc, 64 ch4-loops)

Row 5: As Row 3. (130 sts)

Rows 6–11: Rpt Rows 2–5 once more, then rpt Rows 2–3 once more. (130 sts)

Fasten off securely and weave in ends.

2. CLASP

DISC A

Ch2.

Rnd 1: 6sc in second ch from hook, slst into first sc. (6 sts)

Rnd 2: Ch1, 2sc in every stitch around, slst to first sc. (12 sts)

Rnd 3: Ch1, 1ws in first st, 2ws in next st *1ws, 2ws in next st*, rpt from * to * around, slst into first ws. (18 sts)

Rnd 4: Ch1, 2ws into first st, 2ws, *2ws in next st, 2ws*, rpt from * to * around, slst into first ws. (24 sts)

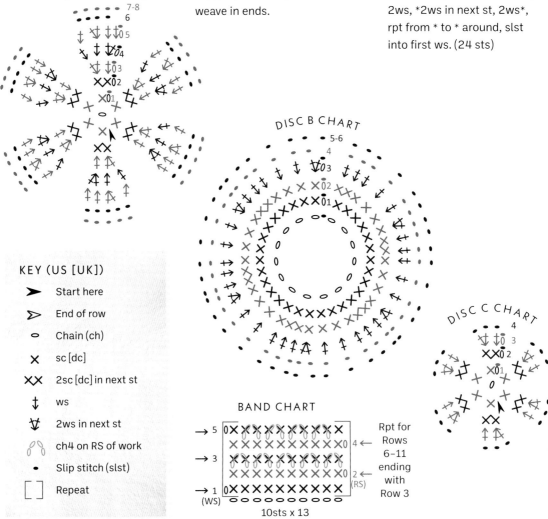

DISC A CHART

DISC B CHART

DISC C CHART

BAND CHART

Rpt for Rows 6–11 ending with Row 3

10sts x 13

KEY (US [UK])

➤ Start here

▷ End of row

○ Chain (ch)

✕ sc [dc]

✕✕ 2sc [dc] in next st

↥ ws

⋎ 2ws in next st

 ch4 on RS of work

• Slip stitch (slst)

[ ] Repeat

Rnd 5: Ch1, 1ws in first st, 1ws, 2ws in next st, 1ws, *2ws, 2ws in next st, 1ws*, rpt from * to * around, slst into first ws. (30 sts)

Rnds 6–8: Slst around.

Fasten off securely, leaving a 10cm/4in tail.

DISC B

Ch15, slst into first ch to form a ring.

Rnd 1: Ch1, 30sc into ring, slst into first sc. (30 sts)

Rnd 2: Ch1, 1sc into first st, 3sc, 2sc in next st, *4sc, 2sc in next st*, rpt from * to * around, slst into first sc. (36 sts)

Rnd 3: Ch1, 2ws in first st, 5ws, *2ws in next st, 5ws*, rpt from * to * around, slst into first ws. (42 sts)

Rnds 4–6: Slst around.

Fasten off securely, leaving a 10cm/4in tail.

DISC C

Ch2, leaving a 10cm/4in tail.

Rnd 1: 6sc in second ch from hook, slst into first sc. (6 sts)

Rnd 2: Ch1, 2sc in first st, 2sc in every st around, slst into first sc. (12 sts)

Rnd 3: Ch1 and 1ws in first st, 2ws in next st, *1ws, 2ws in next st*, rpt from * to * around, slst into first ws. (18 sts)

Rnd 4: Slst around.

Fasten off securely, and weave in end.

FINISHING

To make the clasp, attach one edge of Disc B to one end of the Band using the tail and a tapestry needle. Stitch Discs A and C together in the same way, then fasten Disc C to the other end of the Band through the centre, allowing Disc A to extend from the end of the belt.

Fasten off securely and weave in ends.

PART 2

HOMEWARES

11

RECTANGULAR CUSHION

This beautiful waffle-pattern cushion is created by using a two-colour, three-stitch design, combining double and front post treble stitches, and slip stitches. It's ideal for use inside and outdoors. Add some swish to your garden furniture, or even make an extra-large one for sitting on outside!

YOU WILL NEED

- Yarn: Raffia Viscose
- MC: 90g; approx 198m/216.5yds
- CC: 30g; approx 66m/72.25yds
- Crochet hook: 3mm (No US equivalent – use C2 or D3/UK: 11)
- Tapestry needle
- Scissors
- 25 x 30cm/9.75 x 11.75in cushion pad

GAUGE

19 dc and 6 rows
    = 10 x 10cm/4 x 4in
12 rows of Waffle pattern
    (Rnds 4 and 5) = 10cm/4in

STITCHES

US	UK
ch	ch
slst	slst
dc	tr

Special stitches (see pages 119–121 for tutorials).

FPsc	FPdc
FPtr	FPdtr

FINAL SIZE

Height: 26cm/10.25in
Width: 30cm/12in

SPECIAL NOTES

The Pattern begins with a chain. The first round is worked up one side of the chain, then back down the opposite side. You will then work in joined rounds. Ch3 at the beginning of Rnd 3 doesn't count as a stitch. FPsc with ch3 at the beginning of Rnd 5 counts as the first tr.

To make a higher cushion, increase the foundation chain by multiples of 5. Each 5 sts measures approximately 2.5cm/1in. To make it wider, simply work more repeats of the 2-row Waffle pattern.

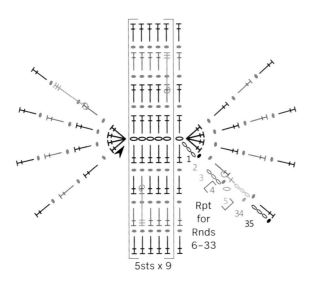

5sts x 9

Rpt for Rnds 6–33

KEY (US [UK])

➤	Start here
o	Chain (ch)
〒	dc [tr]
⩊	4 dc [tr] in next st
ʃ	FPsc [FPdc]
₮	FPtr [FPdtr]
•	Slip stitch (slst)
[ ]	Repeat
■■	MC
■■	CC

PATTERN

Using MC, ch51.

Rnd 1: 4dc in fourth ch from hook, 46dc, 4dc in next ch, turn to work along the opposite side of the chain, 46dc, slst into first dc. (100 sts)

Join CC.

Rnd 2: (CC) Slst around, slst into top of first dc from Rnd 1.

Rnd 3: (CC) Ch3, 1dc in first st, (MC) 4dc, *(CC) 1dc, (MC) 4dc*, rpt from * to * around, slst into first dc.

Rnd 4: (CC) Slst around, slst into top of first st from last rnd.

Rnd 5: (CC) [Ch1, 1FPsc around first st, ch3] (counts as first FPtr), (MC) 4dc, *(CC) 1FPtr, (MC) 4dc*, rpt from * to * around, (CC) slst into top of ch3.

Rnds 6-33: Rpt Rnds 4-5 another 14 times

Rnd 34: Rpt Rnd 4.

Rnd 35: (MC) Ch3, 1dc in first st, 1dc in every st around, slst into first dc.

FINISHING

Fasten off securely and weave in ends. Insert your cushion pad and, using a tapestry needle and a length of raffia viscose yarn approximately 80cm/31.5in long, sew the open cushion edge closed.

ORNAMENTAL BAUBLES

Ornamental baubles look great at any time of year, whether you hang them up or keep them in a decorative bowl or jar. These large and small baubles are each worked in two layers – one to cover the ball and provide a base, and an eye-catching lacy top layer.

YOU WILL NEED

- Yarn: Raffia Viscose
- For the Large Bauble:
MC: 30g; approx 66m/72.25yds
CC: 15g; approx 33m/36yds
- For the Small Bauble:
MC: 25g; approx 55m/60yds,
CC: 10g; approx 22m/24yds
- Crochet hook: 3mm
(No US equivalent – use C2
or D3/UK: 11)
- Stitch marker
- 2 balls: 1 with a diameter
of 10cm/4in, 1 with a diameter
of 8cm/3.25in (I suggest

making them using papier-mâché)
- Tapestry needle
- Scissors

GAUGE

16 ws and 18 rows
  = 10 x 10cm/4 x 4in

FINAL SIZE

Large Bauble:
  Diameter 10cm/4in
Small Bauble:
  Diameter 8cm/3.25in

STITCHES

US	UK
ch	ch
slst	slst
sc	dc
dc	tr
hdc	htr
htr	hdtr
tr	dtr

Special stitch (see page 125 for tutorial).

WS	WS

SPECIAL NOTES

Each bauble is made in four pieces – two inner and two outer sections. The two halves of the inner section are sewn together over the ball. The two halves of the outer section are then placed over this and sewn together.

The two inner pieces are worked in spiral rounds without slst to the beginning of the round. The two outer pieces are worked in joined rounds with slst into the beginning of the round.

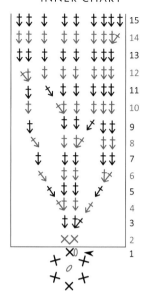

KEY (US [UK])

➤	Start here
○	Chain (ch)
↥	ws
⩔	2ws in next st
✕	sc [dc]
✕✕	2sc [dc] in next st
⊤	hdc [htr]
⩣	1hdc [htr], ch1, 1hdc [htr] in next st
⩣	1hdc [htr], ch3, 1hdc [htr] in next st
⩣	1hdc [htr], ch3, 1hdc [htr] in next st
⊤	dc [tr]
⊤	htr [hdtr]
⊤	tr [dtr]
•	Slip stitch (slst)
[ ]	Repeat
■■	MC
■■	CC

PATTERN

When working in spiral rounds, PM in the first st to keep your place, and move the marker up every round as you work.

LARGE BAUBLE

HALF INNER SECTION (MAKE 2)

Work using MC throughout.

Ch2.

Rnd 1: 6sc in second ch the hook. (6 sts)

Rnd 2: 2sc in every stitch around. (12 sts)

Rnd 3: *2ws in next st, 1ws*, rpt from * to * around. (18 sts)

Rnd 4: *2ws, 2ws in next st*, rpt from * to * around. (24 sts)

Rnd 5: 1ws in every st around.

Rnd 6: *2ws in next st, 3ws*, rpt from * to * around. (30 sts)

Rnd 7: As Rnd 5.

Rnd 8: *2ws, 2ws in next st, 2ws*, rpt from * to * around. (36 sts)

Rnd 9: As Rnd 5.

Rnd 10: *4ws, 2ws in next st, 1ws*, rpt from * to * around. (42 sts)

Rnd 11: As Rnd 5.

Rnd 12: *6ws, 2ws in next st*, rpt from * to * around. (48 sts)

Rnd 13: As Rnd 5.

Rnd 14: *2ws in next st, 7ws*, rpt from * to * around. (54 sts)

Rnd 15: As Rnd 5.

Fasten off securely and weave in ends.

HALF OUTER SECTION (MAKE 2)

Work using CC throughout.

Ch2.

Rnd 1: 6sc in second ch from hook, slst into first sc. (6 sts)

Rnd 2: Ch1, 2sc in first st, 2sc in every st around, slst into first sc. (12 sts)

Rnd 3: Ch1, 1ws in first st, 2ws in next st, *1ws, 2ws in next st*, rpt from * to * around, slst into first ws. (18 sts)

Rnd 4: Ch1, 2ws in first st, 2ws, *2ws in next st, 2ws*, rpt from * to * around, slst into first ws. (24 sts)

Rnd 5: Ch1, 1sc in first st, ch4, sk 2ws, 1dc, ch4, sk 2ws, *1sc, ch4, sk 2ws, 1dc, ch4, sk 2ws*, rpt from * to * around, slst into first sc. (4 sc, 4 dc, 8 ch4-sp)

Rnd 6: Ch8 (counts as 1htr and ch5), 1sc in next dc, ch5, *1htr in next sc, ch5, 1sc in next sc, ch5*, rpt from * to * around, slst into third ch. (4 sc, 4 htr, 8 ch5-sp)

Rnd 7: Ch1, 1sc in first st, ch6, 1tr in next sc, ch6, *1sc in next htr, ch6, 1tr in next sc, ch6*, rpt from * to * around, slst into first sc. (4 sc, 4 tr, 8 ch6-sp)

Rnd 8: Ch10 (first 4-ch counts as 1tr), 1sc in first st, ch6, *1tr in next sc, ch6, 1sc in next tr, ch6*, rpt from * to * around, slst into fourth ch. (4 sc, 4 tr, 8 ch6-sp)

Rnd 9: Ch1, 1sc in first st, ch6, 1htr in next sc, ch6, *1sc, ch6, 1htr, ch6*, rpt from * to * around, slst into first sc. (4 sc, 4 htr, 8 ch6-sp)

Fasten off securely and weave in ends.

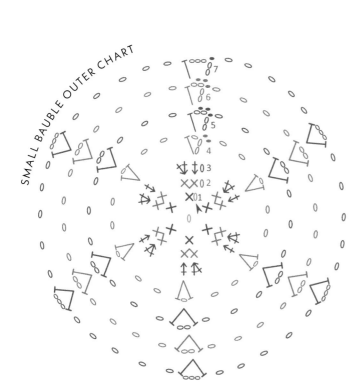

KEY (US [UK])

➤	Start here
o	Chain (ch)
⇟	ws
⋎	2ws in next st
×	sc [dc]
××	2sc [dc] in next st
T	hdc [htr]
▽	1hdc [htr], ch1, 1hdc [htr] in next st
▽	1hdc [htr], ch3, 1hdc [htr] in next st
▽	1hdc [htr], ch3, 1hdc [htr] in next st
†	dc [tr]
‡	htr [hdtr]
‡	tr [dtr]
•	Slip stitch (slst)
[ ]	Repeat
■ ■	MC
■ ■	CC

Rnd 13: *6ws, 2ws in next st*, rpt from * to * around. (48 sts)

Rnd 14: As Rnd 4.

Fasten off, secure and weave in ends.

HALF OUTER SECTION (MAKE 2)

Work using CC throughout.

Ch2.

Rnd 1: 6sc in second ch from the hook, slst into first sc. (6 sts)

Rnd 2: Ch1, 2sc in first st, 2sc in every stitch around, slst into first sc. (12 sts)

SMALL BAUBLE

HALF INNER SECTION (MAKE 2)

Work using MC throughout.

Ch2.

Rnd 1: 6sc in second ch from hook. (6 sts)

Rnd 2: 2sc in every st around. (12 sts)

Rnd 3: *2ws in next st, 1ws*, rpt from * to * around. (18 sts)

Rnd 4: 1ws in every st around. (18 sts)

Rnd 5: *2ws, 2ws in next st*, rpt from * to * around. (24 sts)

Rnd 6: As Rnd 4.

Rnd 7: *2ws in next st, 3ws*, rpt from * to * around. (30 sts)

Rnd 8: As Rnd 4.

SMALL BAUBLE INNER CHART

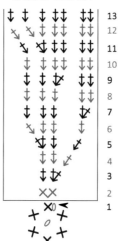

Rnd 9: *2ws, 2ws in next st, 2ws*, rpt from * to * around. (36 sts)

Rnd 10: As Rnd 4.

Rnd 11: *4ws, 2ws in next st, 1ws*, rpt from * to * around. (42 sts)

Rnd 12: As Rnd 4.

Rnd 3: Ch1, 1ws in first st, 2ws in next st, *1ws, 2ws in next st*, rpt from * to * around, slst into first ws. (18 sts)

Rnd 4: Ch3 (counts as 1hdc and ch1), 1hdc in first st, ch2, *sk 2ws, [1hdc, ch1, 1hdc] in next st, ch2*, rpt from * to * around, slst into second ch, slst1 into third ch. (12 hdc, 6 ch1-sp, 6 ch2-sp)

Rnd 5: Ch4 (counts as 1hdc and ch2), 1hdc in same st, ch3, *[1hdc, ch2, 1hdc] into ch of next ch1, ch3*, rpt from * to * around, slst into second ch, slst2. (12 hdc, 6 ch2-sp, 6 ch3-sp)

Rnd 6: Ch4 (counts as 1hdc and ch2), 1hdc in same st, ch4 *[1hdc, ch2, 1hdc] in second ch of next ch2, ch4*, rpt from

* to * around, slst into second ch, slst2. (12 hdc, 6 ch2-sp, 6 ch4-sp)

Rnd 7: Ch5 (counts as 1hdc and ch3), 1hdc in same st, ch5, *[1hdc, ch3, 1hdc] in second ch of next ch2, ch5*, rpt from * to * around, slst into second ch. (12 hdc, 6 ch3-sp, 6 ch5-sp)

FINISHING (BOTH BAUBLES)

Slip both pieces of the inner layer onto to your ball. Using MC, sew the two pieces together as follows: insert your yarn needle into a stitch on the side of piece 1 and then a stitch on the side of piece 2 around, gently stretching each piece as you go to even out the shaping. Repeat the process for the external layer, using CC.

If you want to hang your baubles, use a crochet hook to pull a piece of raffia through the top of each one, and tie to make a loop.

14

LACE TABLECLOTH

A simple, pretty openwork pattern in the round is the basis of this decorative tablecloth. The repeating motif of chain spaces and picot stitches creates a classic lacy design, and you can keep working the rounds until it's the size you need.

YOU WILL NEED

◈ Yarn: Raffia Viscose (60g; approx 132m/144.25yds)
◈ Crochet hook: 3mm (No US equivalent – use C2 or D3/UK: 11)
◈ Tapestry needle
◈ Scissors

GAUGE

16 ws and 18 rows
= 10 x 10cm/4 x 4in

FINAL SIZE

Diameter: 65cm/25.5in

STITCHES

US	UK
ch	ch
slst	slst
sc	dc
hdc	htr
tr	dtr
dtr	trtr
trtr	dtrtr

Special stitch (see page 115 for tutorial).

ws	ws
ch3-picot	ch3-picot

SPECIAL NOTES

Rnds 1–5 are worked in joined rounds with slst to the beginning of the round. Ch1 at the beginning of the round doesn't count as a stitch. From Rnd 6 onwards the pattern is worked in joined rounds, but without slst to the beginning of the round.

As you work, I suggest ironing the tablecloth to set the shape of the sections worked – it is much easier to do this as you go along, rather than to try and shape it at the end!

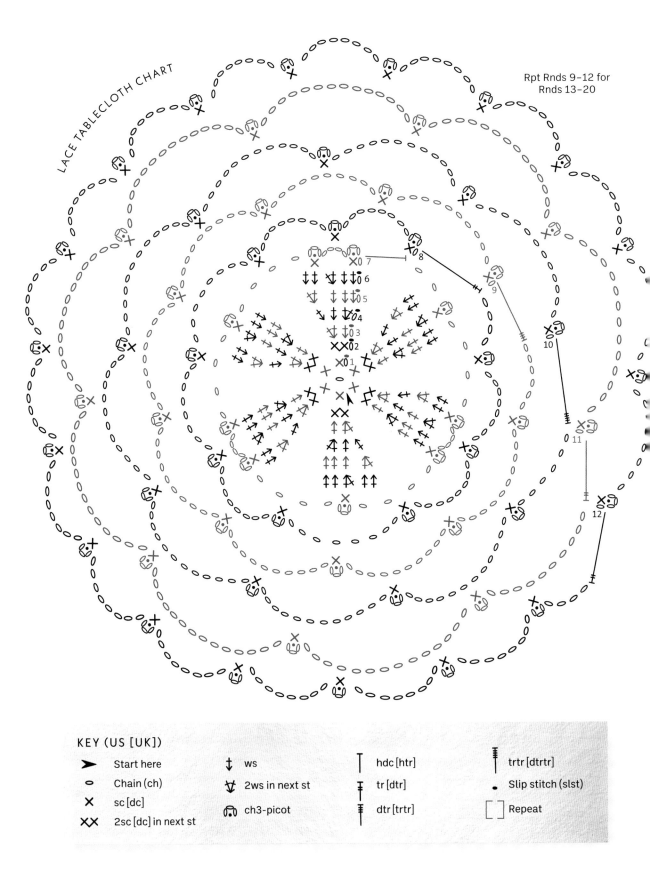

LACE TABLECLOTH CHART

Rpt Rnds 9–12 for Rnds 13–20

KEY (US [UK])

➤	Start here	↕ ws	❘ hdc [htr]	trtr [dtrtr]
○	Chain (ch)	⋎ 2ws in next st	tr [dtr]	• Slip stitch (slst)
✕	sc [dc]	⋔ ch3-picot	dtr [trtr]	[ ] Repeat
✕✕	2sc [dc] in next st			

PATTERN

Ch2.

Rnd 1: 6sc in second ch from hook, slst into first sc. (6 sts)

Rnd 2: Ch1, 2sc in first st, 2sc in every stitch around, slst into first sc. (12 sts)

Rnd 3: Ch1, 1ws in first st, 2ws in next st, *1ws, 2ws in next st*, rpt from * to * around, slst into first ws. (18 sts)

Rnd 4: Ch1, 2ws in first st, 2ws, *2ws in next st, 2ws*, rpt from * to * around, slst to join. (24 sts)

Rnd 5: Ch1, 1ws in first st, 2ws, 2ws in next st, *3ws, 2ws in next st*, rpt from * to * around, slst into first ws. (30 sts)

Rnd 6: Ch1, 1ws in first st, 1ws, 2ws in next st, 2ws *2ws, 2ws in next st, 2ws*, rpt from * to * around, slst into first ws. (36 sts)

Rnd 7: Ch1, 1sc in first st, ch3-picot, ch4, sk 3ws, *1sc, ch3-picot, ch4, sk 3ws*, rpt from * to * another 6 times, 1sc, ch3-picot, ch2, sk 3ws, 1hdc (counts as ch2) into first sc. (9 ch4-sp)

Rnd 8: Ch1, 1sc in first st, ch3-picot *ch8, 1sc in next ch4-sp, ch3-picot*, rpt from * to * another 7 times, ch4, 1tr (counts as ch4) into first sc. (9 ch8-sp)

Rnd 9: Ch1, 1sc in first st, ch3-picot, *ch10, 1sc in next

ch8-sp, ch3-picot*, rpt from * to * another 7 times, ch5, 1dtr (counts as ch5) into first sc. (9 ch10-sp)

Rnd 10: Ch1, 1sc in first st, ch3-picot, *ch12, 1sc in next ch10-sp, ch3-picot*, rpt from * to * another 7 times, ch6, 1trtr (counts as ch6) into first sc. (9 ch12-sp)

Rnd 11: Ch1, 1sc in first st, ch3-picot, *ch14, 1sc in next ch12-sp, ch3-picot*, rpt from * to * another 7 times, ch10, 1tr (counts as ch4) into the first sc. (9 ch14-sp)

Rnd 12: Ch1, 1sc in first st, ch3-picot, *ch8, [1sc, ch3-picot, ch8, 1sc, ch3-picot] in

next ch14-sp*, rpt from * to * another 7 times, ch8, 1sc in next ch14-sp, ch3-picot, ch4, 1tr (counts as ch4) into first sc. (18 ch8-sp)

Rnds 13–16: Rpt Rnds 9–12 once more, repeating the * to * sections another 16 times before joining to first st. (36 ch8-sp)

Rnds 17–20: Rpt Rnds 9–12 once more, repeating the * to * sections another 34 times before joining to first st. (72 ch8-sp)

Fasten off securely and weave in ends.

15

HANGING BASKET

This lovely basket is perfect for trailing plants, or for easy-to-reach storage. It uses raffia paper string worked in waistcoat stitch for a sturdy base, then in a pretty chained latticework pattern around the body, and it's finished off with double crochet for a strong handle.

YOU WILL NEED

- Yarn: Raffia Paper String (100g; approx 150m/164yds)
- Crochet hook: 3mm (No US equivalent – use C2 or D3/UK: 11)
- Stitch marker
- Tapestry needle
- Scissors

GAUGE

16 ws and 18 rows
    = 10 x 10cm/4 x 4in
16 dc and 7 rows
    = 10 x 10cm/4 x 4in
4 rows of lattice pattern
    (Rnds 4–7) = 6cm/2.5in

STITCHES

US	UK
ch	ch
slst	slst
sc	dc
dc	tr
tr	dtr

Special stitch (see page 125 for tutorial).

US	UK
ws	ws

FINAL SIZE

Height including handle:
    27.5cm/10.75in
Diameter of the base:
    17cm/6.75in

SPECIAL NOTES

The Pattern has three parts:

1. Base
2. Body
3. Handle

The Base and Handle are worked in spiral rounds without slst to the beginning of the round.

The Body is worked in a mix of spiral rounds and joined rounds, with and without slst to the beginning of the round.

Each piece is worked consecutively – there is no need to bind off between sections.

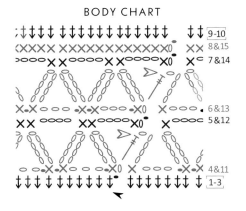

BASE CHART

14
13
12
11
10
9
8
7
6
5
4
3
2
1

BODY CHART

9-10
8 & 15
7 & 14
6 & 13
5 & 12
4 & 11
1-3

PATTERN

When working in spiral rounds, PM in the first st to keep your place, and move the marker up every round as you work.

1. BASE

Ch2.

Rnd 1: 6sc into the second ch from the hook, slst to first sc. (6 sts)

Rnd 2: 2sc in every stitch around. (12 sts)

Rnd 3: *1ws, 2ws in next st*, rpt from * to * around. (18 sts)

Rnd 4: *2ws in next st, 2ws*, rpt from * to * around. (24 sts)

Rnd 5: *3ws, 2ws in next st*, rpt from * to * around. (30 sts)

Rnd 6: *2ws in next st, 4ws*, rpt from * to * around. (36 sts)

Rnd 7: *2ws, 2ws in next st, 3ws*, rpt from * to * around. (42 sts)

Rnd 8: *4ws, 2ws in next st, 2ws*, rpt from * to * around. (48 sts)

Rnd 9: *6ws, 2ws in next st, 1ws*, rpt from * to * around. (54 sts)

Rnd 10: *8ws, 2ws in next st*, rpt from * to * around. (60 sts)

Rnd 11: *2ws in next st, 9ws*, rpt from * to * around. (66 sts)

Rnds 12: *2ws, 2ws in next st, 8ws*, rpt from * to * around. (72 sts)

Rnd 13: *4ws, 2ws in next st, 7ws*, rpt from * to * around. (78 sts)

Rnd 14: *6ws, 2ws in next st, 6ws*, rpt from * to * around. (84 sts)

2. BODY

Rnds 1–3: 1ws in every st around. At the end of Rnd 3, slst into first ws. (84 sts)

Rnd 4: Ch1, 1sc in first st, ch9, slst in same st, *ch3, sk 4, [1sc, ch9, slst in same st] twice*, rpt from * to * to last 5 sts, 1sc, ch9, slst in same st, ch3, sk 4, [1sc, ch5, 1tr (counts as ch4)] into first sc. (14 ch3-sp, 28 ch9-sp)

Rnd 5: Ch1, 1sc in first st, ch4, *[1sc in fifth ch of ch9] twice, ch4*, rpt from * to * final 9ch-sp, 1sc in fifth ch of ch9, slst into first sc. (28 sc, 14 ch4-sp)

Rnd 6: Ch1, 1sc in first st, ch9, slst in same st, ch3, *[1sc into next st, ch9, slst in same st] twice, ch3*, rpt from * to * to last st, [1sc, ch5, 1tr] into first sc. (14 ch-3sp, 28 ch9-sp)

Rnd 7: As Rnd 5.

Rnd 8: Ch1, 1sc in first st, 4sc in next ch4-sp, 1sc *1sc, 4sc in next ch4-sp, 1sc*, rpt from * to * around, slst into first sc. (84 sts)

Rnds 9–10: 1ws in every st around.

Rnds 11–15: Rpt Rnds 4–8 once more.

3. HANDLE

Rnd 1: Ch3, 1dc in first st, 24dc, 6ws, ws2tog, [12ws, ws2tog] twice, 6ws, 17dc, slst into first dc. (81 sts)

Rnd 2: Ch3, dc1 in first st, 24dc, 3ws, ws2tog, 7ws, ws2tog, 11ws, ws2tog, 12ws, 17dc, slst into first dc. (78 sts)

Rnd 3: Ch3, 1dc in first st, ch16, sk 4dc, 20dc, 6ws, ws2tog, 10ws, ws2tog, 11ws, ws2tog, 3ws, 17dc, slst into first dc. (71 sts, 1 ch16-sp)

Rnd 4: Ch3, 1dc in first st, 20dc in ch16-sp, 20dc, 33ws, 17dc, slst into first dc. (91 sts)

Rnds 5–7: Slst around.

Fasten off securely and weave in ends.

16

FLOWERPOT BASKET

This basket has many possible uses, but I love to use mine to hold my flowerpots. The mesh pattern on the body allows for the contents to be visible, so selecting a pot in a contrasting colour is really effective. Although it's quite large, this basket is light and uses surprisingly little yarn.

YOU WILL NEED

- Yarn: Raffia Paper String (50g; approx 75m/82yds)
- Crochet hook: 3mm (No US equivalent – use C2 or D3/UK: 11)
- Stitch marker
- Tapestry needle
- Scissors

GAUGE

16 ws and 18 rows = 10 x 10cm/4 x 4in

6 repeats of Mesh pattern (Body Rnd 8) = 11.5cm/4.5in

STITCHES

US	UK
ch	ch
slst	slst
sc	dc
dc	tr

Special stitches (see pages 119–125 for tutorials).

ws	ws
FPsc	FPdc
FPtr	FPdtr

FINAL SIZE

Total height: 23.5cm/9.25in
Diameter of the base: 18cm/7in

SPECIAL NOTES

This Pattern has three parts:

1. Base
2. Body
3. Handles

The Base is worked in spiral rounds without slst to the beginning of the round.

The Body is worked in a mix of spiral rounds and joined rounds, with and without slst to the beginning of the round.

The Handles are worked in spiral rounds without slst to the beginning of the round.

Each piece is worked consecutively – there is no need to bind off between sections.

BASE CHART

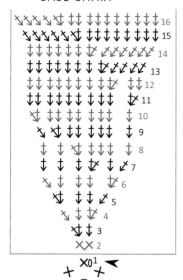

BODY CHART

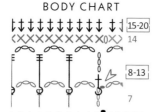

KEY (US [UK])

➤	Start here
➢	End of rnd
o	Chain (ch)
↥	ws
⩔	2ws in next st
✕	sc [dc]
✕✕	2sc [dc] in next st
↥	FPsc [FPdc]
Ꝋ	FPtr [FPdtr]
•	Slip stitch (slst)
[ ]	Repeat

PATTERN

When working in spiral rounds, PM in the first st to keep your place, and move the marker up every round as you work.

1. BASE

Ch2.

Rnd 1: 6sc in second ch from hook, slst into the first sc. (6 sts)

Rnd 2: 2sc in every st around. (12 sts)

Rnd 3: *1ws, 2ws in next st*, rpt from * to * around. (18 sts)

Rnd 4: *2ws in next st, 2ws*, rpt from * to * around. (24 sts)

Rnd 5: *3ws, 2ws in next st*, rpt from * to * around. (30 sts)

Rnd 6: *2ws in next st, 4ws*, rpt from * to * around. (36 sts)

Rnd 7: *2ws, 2ws in next st, 3ws*, rpt from * to * around. (42 sts)

Rnd 8: *4ws, 2ws in next st, 2ws*, rpt from * to * around. (48 sts)

Rnd 9: *6ws, 2ws in next st, 1ws*, rpt from * to * around. (54 sts)

Rnd 10: *8ws, 2ws in next st*, rpt from * to * around. (60 sts)

Rnd 11: *2ws in next st, 9ws*, rpt from * to * around. (66 sts)

Rnd 12: *2ws, 2ws in next st, 8ws*, rpt from * to * around. (72 sts)

Rnd 13: *4ws, 2ws in next st, 7ws*, rpt from * to * around. (78 sts)

Rnd 14: *6ws, 2ws in next st, 6ws*, rpt from * to * around. (84 sts)

Rnd 15: *8ws, 2ws in next st, 5ws*, rpt from * to * around. (90 sts)

Rnd 16: *10ws, 2ws in next st, 4ws*, rpt from * to * around. (96 sts)

2. BODY

Rnds 1–6: 1ws in every st around. At the end of Rnd 6, slst into first ws. (96 sts)

Rnd 7: Ch6 (counts as 1dc, ch3), sk next 2 ws, *1dc, ch3, sk 2ws*, rpt from * to * around, slst into third ch. (32 dc, 32 ch3-sp)

Rnd 8: 1FPsc around first st, ch6 (counts as 1FPtr, ch3), *1FPtr around next dc, ch3*, rpt from * to * around, slst into third ch. (32 FPtr, 32 ch3-sp)

Rnds 9–13: Rpt Rnd 8 another 5 times.

Rnd 14: Ch1, 1sc in first st, 2sc in next ch3-sp, *1sc, 2sc in next ch3-sp*, rpt from * to * around. (96 sts)

Rnds 15–20: 1ws in every st around. (96 sts)

3. HANDLES

Rnd 1: 1ws, ch20, sk 10ws, 38ws, ch20, sk 10ws, 37ws. (116 sts)

Rnd 2: 1ws, 30sc in next ch20-sp, 38ws, 30sc in next ch20-sp, 37ws. (136 sts)

Rnds 3–4: 1ws in every st around.

Rnds 5–7: Slst around.

Fasten off securely and weave in ends.

17

OVAL BASKET

This basket only uses only two stitches – single crochet and waistcoat stitch – but its simplicity is its charm. I use mine to keep my beloved crochet hooks in, but you can use it to tidy away anything, from charging cables to house keys.

YOU WILL NEED

🌀 Yarn: Raffia Paper String (105g; approx 157.5m/172.25yds)
🌀 Crochet hook: 3mm (No US equivalent – use C2 or D3/UK: 11)
🌀 Stitch marker
🌀 Tapestry needle
🌀 Scissors

GAUGE

16 ws and 18 rows
= 10 x 10cm/4 x 4in

FINAL SIZE

Height with lid: 11cm/4.25in
Width: 5.5cm/2.25in
Length: 22cm/8.75in

STITCHES

US	UK
ch	ch
slst	slst
sc	dc

Special stitch (see page 125 for tutorial).

ws	ws

SPECIAL NOTES

The pattern has three parts:

1. Base
2. Lid
3. Handle

The base and lid are worked in spiral rounds without slst to the beginning of the round. The handle is worked in rows.

BASE CHART

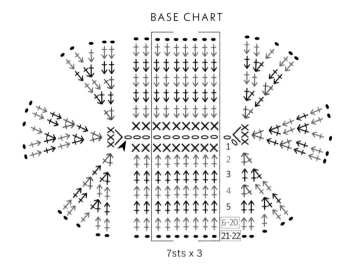

7sts x 3

LID CHART

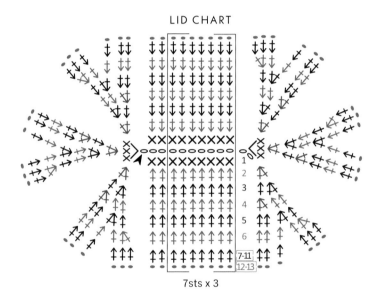

7sts x 3

KEY (US [UK])

➤ Start here
○ Chain (ch)
✕ sc [dc]
⋁⋁⋁ 3sc [3dc] in next st
⋁ 2ws in next st
↨ ws
• Slip stitch (slst)
[ ] Repeat

PATTERN

When working in spiral rounds, PM in the first st to keep your place, and move the marker up every round as you work.

1. BASE

Ch26.

Rnd 1: 3sc in second ch from hook, 23sc, 3sc in next ch, turn to work along the opposite side of the chain, 23sc. (52sc)

Rnd 2: *[2ws in next st] 3 times, 23ws*, rpt from * to * once more. (58 sts)

Rnd 3: *[1ws, 2ws in next st] 3 times, 23ws*, rpt from * to * once more. (64 sts)

Rnd 4: *[2ws in next st, 2ws] 3 times, 23ws*, rpt from * to * once more. (70 sts)

Rnd 5: *[2ws, 2ws in next st, 1ws] 3 times, 23ws*, rpt from * to * once more. (76 sts)

Rnds 6–20: 1ws in every st around.

Rnds 21–22: Slst around.

Fasten off securely and weave in ends.

2. LID

Ch26

Rnds 1–5: Work as for Base.

Rnd 6: *[4ws, 2ws in next st] 3 times, 23ws*, rpt from * to * once more. (82 sts)

Rnds 7–11: 1ws in every st around.

Rnds 12–13: Slst around.

3. HANDLE

Ch16, leaving a long tail at each end. (You will use this to attach the handle to the lid.)

Row 1: 1sc in second ch from hook, 14sc, turn. (15 sts)

Rows 2–4: Ch1, 1sc in first st, 14sc, turn.

Fasten off. Using a tapestry needle and the tails at each end of the chain attach the handle to the lid, placing each end 5cm/2in either side of the central point.

18

RHOMBUS BASKET

This attractive basket uses waistcoat stitch and spike stitch in two
colours to create a pattern of diamonds around the outside. It's very simple,
yet really eye-catching, and will look fantastic wherever you put it.

YOU WILL NEED

- Yarn: Raffia Paper String
- MC: 45g; approx
67.5m/73.75yds
- CC: 85g; approx
127.5m/139.5yds
- Crochet hook: 3mm
(No US equivalent – use C2
or D3/UK: 11)
- Stitch marker
- Tapestry needle
- Scissors

GAUGE

16 ws and 18 rows
= 10 x 10cm/4 x 4in

FINAL SIZE

Height: 15.5cm/6in
Diameter of the base:
11cm/4.25in

STITCHES

US	UK
ch	ch
slst	slst
sc	dc

Special stitches (see pages
124–125 for tutorials).

ws	ws
SPsc	SPdc

SPECIAL NOTES

The Pattern has three parts:

1. Basket
2. Lid
3. Handle

The basket and lid are worked
in spiral rounds without slst to
the beginning of the round.
    The handle is worked in
rows.

BODY CHART

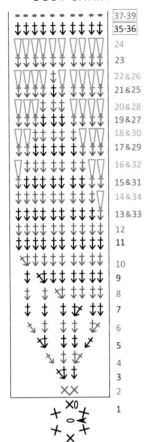

LID CHART

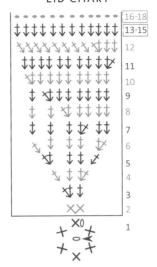

KEY (US [UK])

➤	Start here
o	Chain (ch)
✕	Sc [dc]
✕✕	2sc [dc] in next st
↧	ws
⩔	2ws in next st
▽	SPsc [SPdc]
•	Slip stitch (slst)
[ ]	Repeat
■■	MC
■■	CC

PATTERN

When working in spiral rounds, PM in the first st to keep your place, and move the marker up every round as you work.

1. BASKET

Using MC, ch2.

Rnd 1: 6sc in second ch from hook, slst into first sc. (6 sts)

Rnd 2: 2sc in every stitch around. (12 sts)

Rnd 3: *1ws, 2ws in next st*, rpt from * to * around. (18 sts)

Rnd 4: *2ws in next st, 2ws*, rpt from * to * around. (24 sts)

Rnd 5: *3ws, 2ws in next st*, rpt from * to * around. (30 sts)

Rnd 6: *2ws in next st, 4ws*, rpt from * to * around. (36 sts)

Rnd 7: *2ws, 2ws in next st, 3ws*, rpt from * to * around. (42 sts)

Rnd 8: *4ws, 2ws in next st, 2ws*, rpt from * to * around. (48 sts)

Rnd 9: *6ws, 2ws in next st, 1ws*, rpt from * to * around. (54 sts)

Rnd 10: *8ws, 2ws in next st*, rpt from * to * around. (60 sts)

Rnds 11–12: 1ws in every st around.

Join CC.

Rnd 13: *(CC) 1ws, (MC) 9ws*, rpt from * to * around.

Rnd 14: *(CC) 1SPsc, (MC) 9ws*, rpt from * to * around.

Rnd 15: *(CC) 2ws, (MC) 7ws, (CC) 1ws*, rpt from * to * around.

Rnd 16: *(CC) 2SPsc, (MC) 7ws, (CC) 1SPsc*, rpt from * to * around.

Rnd 17: *(CC) 3ws, (MC) 5ws, (CC) 2ws*, rpt from * to * around.

Rnd 18: *(CC) 3SPsc, (MC) 5ws, (CC) 2SPsc*, rpt from * to * around.

Rnd 19: *(CC) 4ws, (MC) 3ws, (CC) 3ws*, rpt from * to * around.

Rnd 20: *(CC) 4SPsc, (MC) 3ws, (CC) 3SPsc*, rpt from * to * around.

Rnd 21: *(CC) 5ws, (MC) 1ws, (CC) 4ws*, rpt from * to * around.

Rnd 22: *(CC) 5SPsc, (MC) 1ws, (CC) 4SPsc*, rpt from * to * around.

Rnd 23: Using CC, 1ws in every st around.

Rnd 24: Using CC, 1SPsc in every st around.

Rnds 25–26: Rpt Rnds 21–22.

Rnds 27–28: Rpt Rnds 19–20.

Rnds 29–30: Rpt Rnds 17–18.

Rnds 31–32: Rpt Rnds 15–16.

Rnds 33–34: Rpt Rnds 13–14.

Break CC and continue using MC only.

Rnds 35–36: 1ws in every st around.

Rnds 37–39: Slst around.

Fasten off securely and weave in ends.

2. LID

Use CC throughout.

Ch2.

Rnd 1: 6sc in second ch from hook, slst into first sc. (6 sts)

Rnd 2: 2sc in every stitch around. (12 sts)

Rnd 3: *1ws, 2ws in next st*, rpt from * to * around. (18 sts)

Rnd 4: *2ws in next st, 2ws*, rpt from * to * around. (24 sts)

Rnd 5: *3ws, 2ws in next st*, rpt from * to * around. (30 sts)

Rnd 6: *2ws in next st, 4ws*, rpt from * to * around. (36 sts)

Rnd 7: *2ws, 2ws in next st, 3ws*, rpt from * to * around. (42 sts)

Rnd 8: *4ws, 2ws in next st, 2ws*, rpt from * to * around. (48 sts)

Rnd 9: *6ws, 2ws in next st, 1ws*, rpt from * to * around. (54 sts)

Rnd 10: *8ws, 2ws in next st*, rpt from * to * around. (60 sts)

Rnd 11: *2ws in next st, 9ws*, rpt from * to * around. (66 sts)

Rnd 12: *2ws, 2ws in next st, 8ws*, rpt from * to * around. (72 sts)

Rnds 13–15: 1ws in every st around.

Rnds 16–18: Slst around. (72 slst)

Fasten off securely and weave in ends.

3. HANDLE

Ch11, leaving a long tail at each end. (You will use this to attach the handle to the lid.)

Row 1: 1sc in second ch from hook, 1sc in every ch, turn. (10 sts)

Row 2: Ch1, 1sc in first st, 9sc.

Fasten off. Use the tails at the end of the chain and the tapestry needle to attach the handle to the lid. Fold the handle in half and attach each end to the centre of the lid.

Weave in all ends.

19

CONE VASE

This little vase is perfect for displaying dried flowers, grasses or feathers, or just leaving empty as a decoration in itself. It has a wide, stable base, and the waistcoat stitch used throughout gives it plenty of structure. Don't fill it with water, though – it would not last long!

YOU WILL NEED

- Yarn: Raffia Paper String
- MC: 61g; approx 91.50m/100yds
- CC: 12g; approx 18m/19.75yds
- Crochet hook: 3mm (No US equivalent – use C2 or D3/UK: 11)
- Stitch marker
- Tapestry needle
- Scissors

GAUGE

16 ws and 18 rows
= 10 x 10cm/4 x 4in

FINAL SIZE

Height: 16.5cm/6.5in
Diameter of the base: 15cm/6in

STITCHES

US	UK
ch	ch
slst	slst
sc	dc

Special stitch (see page 125 for tutorial).

US	UK
ws	ws

SPECIAL NOTES

The Pattern has two parts:

1. Base
2. Body

Both parts are worked in spiral rounds without slst to the beginning of the round. There is no need to fasten off between each section.

BASE CHART

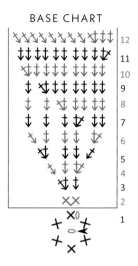

KEY (US [UK])

➤	Start here
○	Chain (ch)
✕	sc [dc]
✕✕	2sc [dc] in next st
↧	2ws in next st
↯	ws
⋔	ws2tog
•	Slip stitch (slst)
[ ]	Repeat
◼◼◼	MC
◼◼◼	CC

BODY CHART

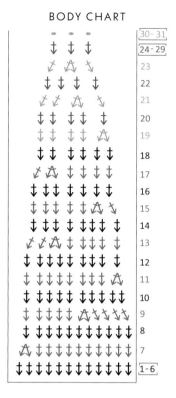

PATTERN

When working in spiral rounds, PM in the first st to keep your place, and move the marker up every round as you work.

1. BASE

Using MC, ch2.

Rnd 1: 6sc in second ch from hook, slst into first sc. (6 sts)

Rnd 2: 2sc in every st around. (12 sc)

Rnd 3: *1ws, 2ws in next st*, rpt from * to * around. (18 sts)

Rnd 4: *2ws in next st, 2ws*, rpt from * to * around. (24 sts)

Rnd 5: *3ws, 2ws in next st*, rpt from * to * around. (30 sts)

Rnd 6: *2ws in next st, 4ws*, rpt from * to * around. (36 sts)

Rnd 7: *2ws, 2ws in next st, 3ws*, rpt from * to * around. (42 sts)

Rnd 8: *4ws, 2ws in next st, 2ws*, rpt from * to * around. (48 sts)

Rnd 9: *6ws, 2ws in next st, 1ws*, rpt from * to * around. (54 sts)

Rnd 10: *8ws, 2ws in next st*, rpt from * to * around. (60 sts)

Rnd 11: *2ws in next st, 9ws*, rpt from * to * around. (66 sts)

Rnd 12: *2ws, 2ws in next st, 8ws*, rpt from * to * around. (72 sts)

2. BODY

Rnds 1–6: 1ws in every st around. (72 sts)

Rnd 7: *10ws, ws2tog*, rpt from * to * around. (66 sts)

Rnd 8 and all even-numbered rounds to Rnd 22: 1ws in every st around.

Rnd 9: *4ws, ws2tog, 5ws*, rpt from * to * around. (60 sts)

Rnd 11: *ws2tog, 8ws*, rpt from * to * around. (54 sts)

Rnd 13: *5ws, ws2tog, 2ws*, rpt from * to * around. (48 sts)

Rnd 15: *1ws, ws2tog, 5ws*, rpt from * to * around. (42 sts)

Rnd 17: *4ws, ws2tog, 1ws*, rpt from * to * around. (36 sts)

Rnd 18: Rpt Rnd 8.

Break MC and join CC.

Rnd 19: *ws2tog, 4ws*, rpt from * to * around. (30 sts)

Rnd 21: *2ws, ws2tog, 1ws*, rpt from * to * around. (24 sts)

Rnd 23: *1ws, ws2tog, 1ws*, rpt from * to * around. (18 sts)

Rnds 24–29: Rpt Rnd 8 another 6 times.

Rnds 30–31: Slst around.

Fasten off securely and weave in ends.

20

FLEXIBLE VASE

The joy of this vase is its malleability. It uses waistcoat stitch throughout to give it structure and stability, but the nature of the stitches means you can mould it into different shapes depending on your mood or where you put the vase. The contrasting rim adds a simple but striking touch.

YOU WILL NEED

⚜ Yarn: Raffia Paper String
⚜ MC: 80g; approx 120m/131.25yds
⚜ CC: 1g; approx 1.50m/1.75yds
⚜ Crochet hook: 3mm (No US equivalent – use C2 or D3/UK: 11)
⚜ Stitch marker
⚜ Tapestry needle
⚜ Scissors

GAUGE

16 ws and 18 rows
= 10 x 10cm/4 x 4in

FINAL SIZE

Height: 17cm/6.75in
Diameter of the base: 10cm/4in

STITCHES

US	UK
ch	ch
slst	slst
sc	dc

Special stitch (see page 125 for tutorial).

US	UK
ws	ws

SPECIAL NOTES

The Pattern has two parts:

1. Base
2. Body

Both parts are worked in spiral rounds without slst to the beginning of the round. There is no need to fasten off between sections.

BASE CHART

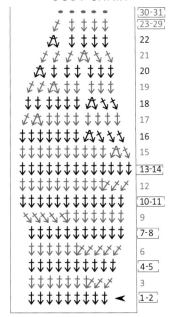

BODY CHART

KEY (US [UK])

➤	Start here
o	Chain (ch)
✕	sc [dc]
✕✕	2sc [dc] in next st
‡	2ws in next st
Ѱ	ws
Ѧ	ws2tog
•	Slip stitch (slst)
[ ]	Repeat
■■ MC	■■ CC

PATTERN

When working in spiral rounds, PM in the first st to keep your place, and move the marker up every round as you work.

1. BASE

Work Base using MC throughout.

Ch2.

Rnd 1: 6sc in second ch from the hook, slst into first sc. (6 sc)

Rnd 2: 1sc in every st around. (12 sc)

Rnd 3: *1ws, 2ws in next st*, rpt from * to * around. (18 sts)

Rnd 4: *2ws in next st, 2ws*, rpt from * to * around. (24 sts)

Rnd 5: *3ws, 2ws in next st*, rpt from * to * around. (30 sts)

Rnd 6: *2ws in next st, 4ws*, rpt from * to * around. (36 sts)

Rnd 7: *2ws, 2ws in next st, w3*, rpt from * to * around. (42 sts)

Rnd 8: *4ws, 2ws in next st, 2ws*, rpt from * to * around. (48 sts)

Rnd 9: *6ws, 2ws in next st, 1ws*, rpt from * to * around. (54 sts)

2. BODY

Rnds 1–2: 1ws in every st around. (54 sts)

Rnd 3: *2ws, 2ws in next st, 6ws*, rpt from * to * around. (60 sts)

Rnds 4–5: Rpt Rnds 1–2.

Rnd 6: *4ws, 2ws in next st, 5ws*, rpt from * to * around. (66 sts)

Rnds 7–8: Rpt Rnds 1–2.

Rnd 9: *6ws, 2ws in next st, 4ws*, rpt from * to * around. (72 sts)

Rnds 10–11: Rpt Rnds 1–2.

Rnd 12: *2ws, 2ws in next st, 9ws*, rpt from * to * around. (78 sts)

Rnds 13–14: Rpt Rnds 1–2.

Rnd 15: *1ws, ws2tog, ws10*, rpt from * to * around. (72 sts)

Rnd 16: *4ws, ws2tog, 6ws*, rpt from * to * around. (66 sts)

Rnd 17: *8ws, ws2tog, 1ws*, rpt from * to * around. (60 sts)

Rnd 18: *2ws, ws2tog, 6ws*, rpt from * to * around. (54 sts)

Rnd 19: *5ws, ws2tog, 2ws*, rpt from * to * around. (48 sts)

Rnd 20: *6ws, ws2tog*, rpt from * to * around. (42 sts)

Rnd 21: *2ws, ws2tog, 3ws*, rpt from * to * around. (36 sts)

Rnd 22: *4ws, ws2tog*, rpt from * to * around. (30 sts)

Rnds 23–29: 1ws in every st around.

Break MC. Work next 2 rnds in CC.

Rnds 30–31: Slst around.

Fasten off securely and weave in ends.

PART 3

SPECIAL STITCHES

CELTIC WEAVE STITCH

The stitch uses Front Post treble stitches (FPtr [FPdtr]). See the tutorial on page 121 for an explanation of this stitch. Celtic Weave stitch is worked across 2 rows: **1.** A front cross row. **2.** A back cross row.

Steps 1 and 2 are the same for both:

1 Sk 2 FPtr, 1FPtr in next st.

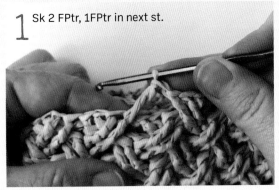

2 1FPtr in next st.

Front cross set steps 3 and 4:

3 Cross in front of sts just made, 1FPtr around first sk st.

4 1FPtr around second sk st.

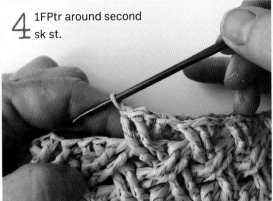

Back cross set steps 3 and 4:

3 Cross behind sts just made, 1FPtr around first sk st.

4 1FPtr around second sk st.

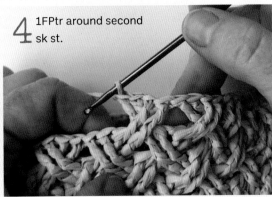

1 Ch3.

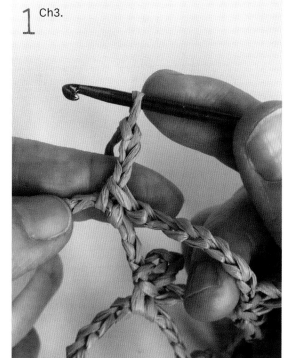

2 Insert your hook in the front loop of the sc before the ch3.

3 Insert your hook in the left leg of the sc (3 loops on hook).

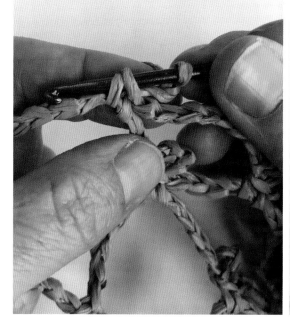

4 Yarn over hook and draw through all loops on the hook.

CHAIN LOOPS STITCH

This stitch is worked across 2 rows – a right side (RS) row and a wrong side (WS) row – and creates loops that create a textured surface on the right side of the fabric.

(RS)

(WS)

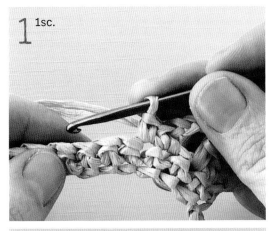

1 1sc.

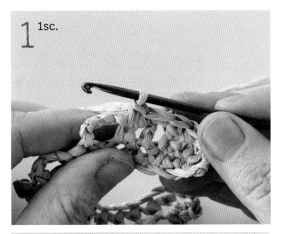

1 1sc.

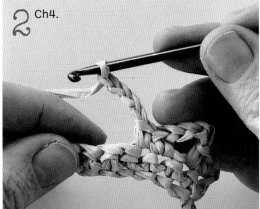

2 Ch4.

2 Keep the chain loops on the RS of your work.

3 1sc into next st.

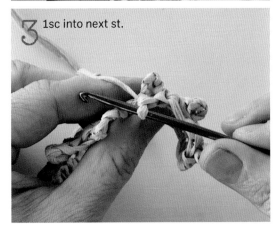

3 1sc into next st.

BEGINNING CROSS-TREBLE CROCHET (BEG CROSS-TR [BEG CROSS-DTR])

This set-up stitch is worked at the beginning of a cross-treble row, establishing the stitch repeat.

1 Ch2.

2 Sk 2 sts, 1dc in next st.

3 Ch5.

4 1dc into 2 loops of dc at the base of ch-5.

CROSS-TREBLE CROCHET (CROSS-TR [CROSS-DTR])

The cross-treble is worked over four stitches and forms an X.

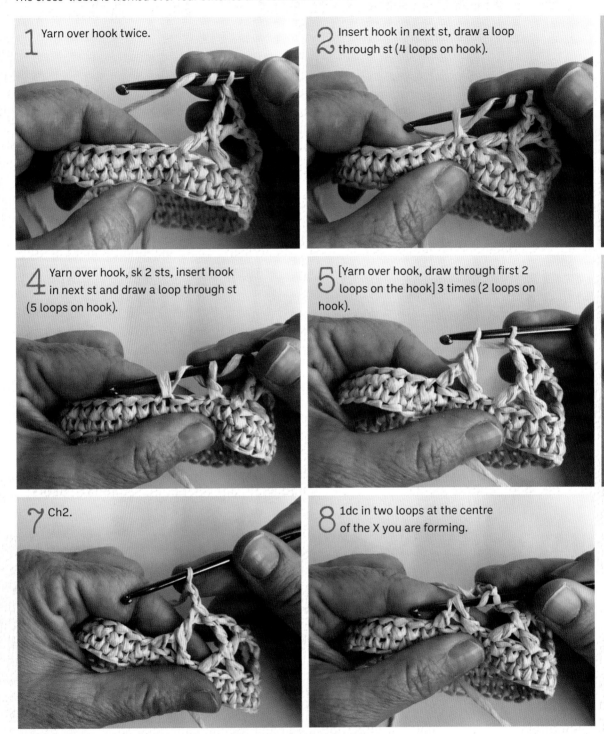

1 Yarn over hook twice.

2 Insert hook in next st, draw a loop through st (4 loops on hook).

4 Yarn over hook, sk 2 sts, insert hook in next st and draw a loop through st (5 loops on hook).

5 [Yarn over hook, draw through first 2 loops on the hook] 3 times (2 loops on hook).

7 Ch2.

8 1dc in two loops at the centre of the X you are forming.

3 Yarn over hook, draw through first 2 loops on the hook (3 loops on hook).

6 Yarn over hook, draw through last 2 loops on the hook.

FRONT POST STITCHES

Front post stitches are worked around the post (body) of the stitch, rather than into the top of the stitch.

FRONT POST SINGLE CROCHET (FPSC [FPDC])

FPsc is shown here worked around a ch-3 from the row below.

1 Insert your hook from front to back, so that st sits in front of hook.

2 Yarn over hook, draw a loop through st (2 loops on hook).

3 Yarn over hook, draw through 2 loops on the hook.

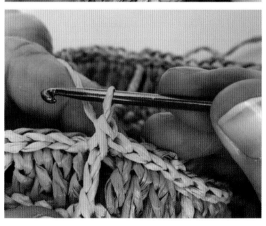

1 Yarn over hook once.

2 Insert your hook from front to back so that st sits in front of hook.

3 Yarn over hook, draw a loop through st (3 loops on hook).

4 Yarn over hook, draw through 3 loops on the hook.

FRONT POST TREBLE CROCHET (FPTR [FPDTR])

1 Yarn over hook twice.

2 Insert your hook from front to back so that st sits in front of hook.

3 Yarn over hook, draw a loop through st (4 loops on hook).

4 [Yarn over hook, draw through first 2 loops on the hook] twice (2 loops on hook).

5 Yarn over hook, draw through 2 loops on the hook.

PUFF PETAL

Each petal is worked across two stitches and finishes with a slip stitch into the second stitch.

1 Ch3.

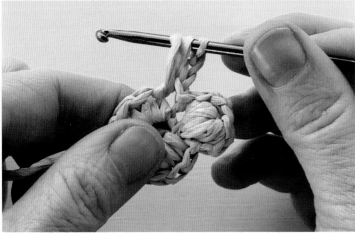

2 Yarn over hook, insert hook in first st, pull through and bring loop up to the same height as the 3-ch (3 loops on hook).

3 Yarn over hook, insert hook in same st, pull through and bring loop up to the same height as the previous loop] twice more (7 loops on hook).

4 Into the next st, [yarn over hook, insert hook in st, pull through and bring loop up to the same height as the previous loop] 3 times (13 loops on hook).

5 Yarn over hook, pull through all loops on hook.

6 Ch3, then slst into the stitch from step 4.

SPIKE STITCH (SPSC [SPDC])

Spike stitch is worked as a single crochet stitch (sc), but into a stitch in a row below the one being worked.

1 Insert hook in top of st below the current row (or row indicated by pattern).

2 Yarn over hook, draw through a loop through st.

3 Bring loop up to the height of the current row.

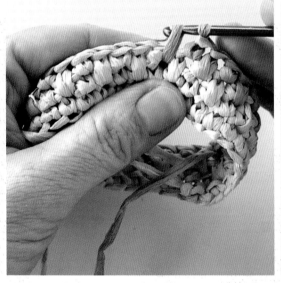

4 Yarn over hook, draw through 2 loops on hook.

WAISTCOAT STITCH (WS [WS])

This stitch is a variation of the single crochet stitch (sc), but instead of working the top of the stitch, you insert your hook through the stitch itself. It creates a sturdy fabric that resembles knitted stocking stitch.

1 Insert your hook into the v-shape in the centre of the st.

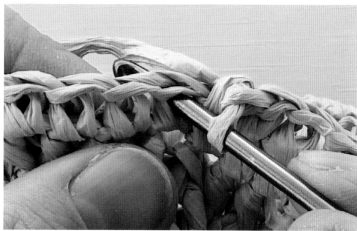

2 Yarn over hook, draw through a loop (2 loops on hook).

3 Yarn over hook, draw through both loops.

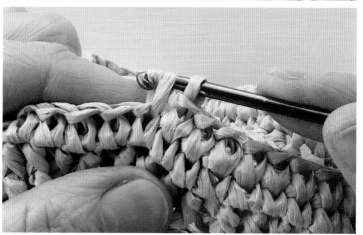

RAFFIA SUPPLIERS

RAFFIA VISCOSE 100%

Borgo de' Pazzi
Piazza Oglio, 49 59013
Montemurlo, Italy
+39 335 302 012
info@borgodepazzi.com
www.borgodepazzi.com

Ice Yarns
www.iceyarns.com

ISPIEofficial
New York, USA
www.etsy.com/shop/
ISPIEofficial

Lane Mondial
Via G. di Vittorio, 4 25125
Brescia, Italy
+39 030 3540161
info@lanemondial.com
www.lanemondial.it

Ophelia
Via Dei Mugnai, 4/6 59100
Prato, Italy
+39 340 993 0494
info@opheliaitaly.com
www.opheliaitaly.com

SistersnaturaTR
www.etsy.com/uk/shop/
SistersnaturaTR

Sweet Pea Dolls
www.sweetpeadolls.co.uk

RAFFIA PAPER STRING

Ferpa
180 High Road
IG1 1LR, Ilford
London, United Kingdom
info@ferpa.co.uk
www.ferpa.co.uk

Ganxxet
2624 NW 72nd Avenue
Miami
Florida, USA
hello@ganxxet.com
www.ganxxet.com

Hobbii
www.hobbii.co.uk

Max + Herb
www.maxandherb.com

ORA Fabulous Fibres
39 Hope Street
Perth, Australia
+61 400 651 201
hello@orafabulousfibres.com
www.orafabulousfibres.com

Paperphine
www.paperphine.com

Etsy
www.etsy.com
Suggested shops:
bg7day
CrafterClowex
GMBBoutique
KreativGarne
MTCraftSupplies
StudioSunnyThreads
STYLEMODA
TheRopesStore
Vollen Yarn
Yarnofanatolia
YarnsVarious

NB: If it is not clear which type of paper raffia is on offer, please contact the supplier to find out and make sure you order the string type and not the single thread. Raffia paper string can also be found as raffia paper cord, 2ply or twine.

Please note that we have not tried all of these yarns. The list is based on the information provided by each supplier.

ACKNOWLEDGEMENTS

This book wouldn't have been possible in this period of my life without the support (both technical and emotional) of my friend Hara Giannakopoulou, who stood by me from day one of this book-writing adventure, offering her professional insight and publishing experience, but also her sense of humour. Thank you, Hara.

A very special thanks to all the people who contributed in one or more ways to the making of the book:

Maria Siorba, my photographer, for her images that are always so full of tenderness and affection.

Myrsini Tzavara, my model, for her youthful beauty that filled the images of the book.

Graciella Feller, for her hospitality one cold winter morning, Vagelis Jannis for our precious collaboration, Artemis Loi and Vicky Christoforidou for their advice.

Clare Martelli and Caroline Guillet for their kindness, trust, patience and support throughout this journey. Also, tech editor Rachael Prest for making me a more meticulous crocheter, designer Austin Taylor and everybody else at Herbert Press for making this book happen.

Thanks to all the people who have given me their precious feedback, bought my patterns or even shared a truthful comment concerning my work.

Last but not least, Yiannis Lois, for always reminding me who I want to be and making sure this happens.

Without you this book wouldn't exist.